The Dark Clouds at Work:

Depression in the workplace and what to do about it
(2nd Edition)

By

Dr. Darryl Cross

Disclaimer

This publication is designed to provide accurate and authoritative information with regard to the subject matter covered. It is sold with the understanding that the author is not engaged in rendering legal, accounting or financial advice of any kind. If legal advice or other professional assistance is required, the services of a competent professional in the appropriate area should be sought.

The author denies any liability for incidental or consequential damages resulting from the use of the information in this book. This book is designed to assist with generating and exploring various options for assisting people in the workplace who might be considered depressed. It does not make decisions for the individual, but provides a range of options to be considered. No responsibility is accepted for any liabilities resulting from the actions of any parties involved.

By the same Author:

Available on www.DrDarryl.com

"You're a New Leader: So Now What?"

"Listen Up Now! How to Increase Profit and Growth in Business by Really Listening to Your Clients & Customers"

"In Pursuit of Success and Happiness: A Practical Guide"

"How to Stop Your Self-Sabotage: Steps to Increase Your Self-Confidence"

"Teenager Trouble-Shooting: How to Stop Your Adolescent Driving You Crazy"

"Growing up Children: How To Get 5 – 12 Year Olds To Behave & Do As They're Told"

Cover design by Mykhailo Uvarov

Published by Crossways Publishing (2nd Edition)

ISBN: 0-9806101-8-4
ISBN-13: 978-0-9806101-8-5

Visit www.DrDarryl.com to order additional copies

Testimonials

"Dr. Cross makes a compelling case for the importance of managing depression in the workplace. He clearly lays out the staggering cost implications, and his thorough analysis makes one wonder why so many leading companies fail to provide programs to help address workplace depression. With so much at stake, clearly more companies need to include mental well-being in their overall approach to employee wellness."

Paul Kessler, Managing Director, The Syncretics Group, USA, and Co-author of *Leading at the Edge: Leadership Lessons from the Extraordinary Saga of Shackleton's Antarctic Expedition*

"One thing you learn in managing organisations is that every one is watching. The culture in an organisation will be determined by how people are treated. When someone in the workforce is suffering depression it is important to both the individual who has depression and those around them that the situation is managed professionally.

This book asserts the reality that depression is alive in organisations and that we are all likely to encounter someone with depression in our working career. It brings a heightened awareness of the issues of depression to the reader. The new learning for me was that depression can be professionally managed in the work force and in fact, this is the right place to manage it."

John Moller, Managing Director, Exego Group, Mulgrave, Victoria, Australia

"With 10-20% of people in our workplace suffering depression at some stage, Dr. Cross' book is a timely and valuable resource for managers seeking a practical guide on how to recognize it, and more importantly, what to do about it."

Rev. Dr. Nick Hawkes, Retired Pastor, Rivergate Christian Community, Athelstone, South Australia

"I'm always amazed at Darryl's ability to read and interpret the moods and changes in the workplace. Once again he has nailed what is clearly a huge concern for people leading businesses, how do you look after your people in incredibly challenging times?

The workplace is going through change at a pace not seen before and employees are under more pressure, tighter deadlines, higher customer expectations and are connected 24 hours a day, 7 days a week. People are clearly struggling. Darryl's book is incredibly insightful and filled with great ideas to find joy and a way forward. It's a must read for all employers and employees."

Damien Eves, Executive Coach, The Horton Program, Perth, Western Australia

"The covid operational challenges have been industry wide and it seems that just as managers and leaders have come to terms with these challenges, and begin to focus on their core business, another grey cloud has been rolling into view, namely, mental health. Managers and leaders are often well versed at solving operational or financial issues, often seeing them coming before they bite. Mental health however, hides in plain sight, and many of us struggle to know how to approach this challenge.

Darryl's book is a fantastic resource for managers to start to understand mental health and in particular, depression. It provides an informative and practical frame-work to help managers and staff navigate this unfamiliar territory in the workplace. I highly recommend this book for managers or aspirational leaders. It will help you in so many aspects of your professional and personal life. Do yourself and your colleagues a favour and read this book!"

Ashley Burns, General Manager, Living Colour Nursery, Penfield, South Australia

"I have personal experience of how depression can affect people at all levels of business, including the very top, sometimes without them even realizing they have it. As a professional speaker, motivator, business owner and writer, I believe Dr. Cross' book should not only be up there in the 'must haves' of every business owner's bookshelf, but actually in their hands – reading it."

Phil Gosling, Disley, United Kingdom, Author of *Success Engineering*, www.success-engineering.com

"Like many others, today our business is being confronted with mental health issues in a way that we haven't seen previously. Our key focus has always been our core business, but with the growing number of workers turning up with depression and related mental health issues, that focus has shifted.

We've had to quickly learn how to handle these growing mental health challenges and how to best support our people. This book has been a great guide in helping me and our business better understand and support mental health both at home and in our personal lives, I highly recommend it."

David Principessa, General Manager Retail, ABN Group, Docklands, Victoria, Australia

"As an executive coach working with key leaders and their staff, I am finding an alarming and growing number of clients suffering from depression in the work place. The competitive nature of workplaces compels sufferers to keep their condition secret and avoid seeking help. The cost to them, their families, their colleagues and their organisations is a silent and unseen hemorrhage of energy, talent and money.

In "The Dark Clouds At Work" Dr. Cross has effectively provided sufferers of depression and all those who have a stake in their effectiveness, welfare and indeed happiness, a powerful and practical manual to understand, recognise and manage this silent scourge."

Ron Jungalwalla,   Quest Group Australia Pty Ltd, Melbourne, Victoria, Australia

"Post COVID we've seen a noticeable increase in mental health issues amongst our team members within our business. So much so, that mental health generally has become a normalised topic for discussion during our toolbox meetings. Awareness has encouraged us as business owners to provide resources and healthy discussions around mental health and how/where to get help.

Dr Darryl's book has been a great resource for promoting self-awareness of mental health and signs to look out for if we think our colleagues are suffering. Jam packed full of tips and techniques to help ourselves and the people around us."

Penni Donato, Managing Director, Allin Towbars, Richmond, South Australia

"Managers today need a broader skill base to cover not only shareholder and business expectations but to identify, approach and manage staff with underlying mental health issues resulting from the demands of the 21st century.

This is a practical, easy to read book for all managers to help performance manage staff dealing specifically with depression."

Bronwyn Wright, Group Quality Systems Manager, Constellation Wines Australia, Reynella, South Australia

"Depression is a growing global issue that at some point we will all encounter whether in the workplace or in our personal lives. It is a difficult topic to approach in any setting. Dr. Cross does a fantastic job of breaking it down into easy-to-understand solutions for managers. "The Dark Clouds At Work" is a resource that I would recommend to all the Business Advisors that I work with."

Tanya Chapman, North America Regional Manager, Mindshop International, Atlanta, Georgia USA

"I highly recommend this book which was originally published in 2009, however, in the wake of COVID-19, Dr Cross realised an update was needed as staff across the world return to work while managing the after effects of the worldwide pandemic.

Depression can affect every part of the workplace - including the vital bottom line. Dr Cross offers a deep dive into this very real issue to help navigate this often silent pandemic.

Leaders and managers would do well to study this book, which offers solutions to help workers, and offers much needed hope for workers and leaders like me alike. Dr Darryl sure has helped me and my management team and we highly recommend him to help in your business."

Mark Taylor, Chief Executive Officer, ACE Radio Network, Melbourne, Victoria, Australia

"Wow, what a breath of fresh air for all business owners. As a consultant and trainer working with teams and leaders across Australia this book should be a vital part of the leadership tool box.

We witness many organisations and leaders who cannot see the cost and long term suffering of depression in the workplace. Darryl's work has already had massive personal implications for my business and family and now a guide for my customers, what more could I ask for, brilliant."

Mike Boyle, Founder and Senior Consultant, Banjar Group, Melbourne, Victoria, Australia

" 'The Dark Clouds at Work: How to manage depressed staff in the workplace', promises to be a powerful instrument for leaders and managers. Providing a support tool that steps through from identification to proactive support techniques, this book should help us to improve the wellbeing of our peers and those around them and potentially save lives. Assisting with foundational knowledge and strategies for the inevitable moments our team need mental health support."

Sarah Leo, Chief Executive Officer, Resonate Consultants, South Australia

"The statistics showing such a large population of people effected by depression in the workplace shows the need for people to be more aware of the symptoms, causes, treatments and ways to deal with it in the workplace. The examples of real people dealing with this illness throughout the book drives the point home.

Not only does Darryl's work increase your awareness level, but he gives us a practical application intervention model that can be used by any manager to address an issue with an employee."

JoAnn (Cory) Labbie, EdD, CPA, Chief People Officer, Allinial Global, Lawrenceville, Georgia, USA

"Like so many business leaders over the past 40 years, I have seen a rise of depression in the workplace. Often a difficult subject to broach with a staff member or colleague, Dr Darryl Cross masterfully steps us through a process that assists us in managing situations that can arise from depressive behaviours. While the cost of depression to our businesses is considerable, nothing can be more rewarding than being a part of helping a workmate regain a healthier lifestyle."

Gerard McCabe, Founder, Gerard McCabe Jewellers, Adelaide, South Australia

"Depression in the workplace is real and the personal cost to depressed and non-depressed staff alike is just as high as the financial loss it causes many organisations. If you work in a company alongside colleagues, this book is a must read. If you are a manager or leader in a company this book is an ESSENTIAL read!

Every chapter is an eye-opener on what's currently happening, how to identify and more importantly how to correctly deal with this "silent embezzler".

Kevin Enright, Sales Manager, Dale Alcock Homes, Perth Western Australia, and Author of best-selling book "Bricks and Mortar"

Acknowledgements

It was at the end of the MBA class that I was taking on Leadership that one of the students called Bronwyn came up to me and commented in passing that she and her group had thoroughly enjoyed the conversation that we'd all had on depression in the workplace and what to do about it. Although it was a distraction from the text and the Study Guide for the class, she indicated how helpful it had been. It was that night that I woke up with the outline of this book in my head. I scribbled down the various chapter headings on a small pad on the bedside table. That was back in 2009 when the book was first published after the Global Financial Crisis (GFC).

Since then, life has continued to move at a faster rate and become more uncertain and complex with increased change and developments in both our culture and society, our technology, our businesses, our education systems and our way of living. Then came covid-19 which turned everything upside down, created massive change in quick time and where things have not returned to where they were. All this necessitated a re-write of this book.

My thanks goes to all those clients who I have had the privilege of meeting professionally who have taught me so much about their journey and dealing with depression. Thanks too to those who have shared their lessons about how covid impacted their lives. We all have so much to learn.

I am indebted too to my wife Billie who is always there encouraging and supporting and who understands that there are times when I am laptop bound.

Darryl

Foreword

This book, *The Dark Clouds at Work* is timely. Thirty plus years as a psychologist with specialist training and experience in both clinical and organisational psychology study and practice has provided Dr. Darryl Cross with a relatively rare set of skills. He uses these skills in a way which managers should find quite helpful. Over the past decade we have been hearing more and more about depression. We have also been hearing about depression in the workplace. There probably isn't a manager who hasn't heard about depression in the workplace. No doubt many of them have experienced staff about whom they wondered if they were depressed or just having a "bad hair day". This book provides the reader with a lot of information about depression including: its causes, its manifestations, how to identify it, possible treatments, but most importantly it provides the manager with some action steps which can be taken. The book is clearly a road-map for leaders and managers who take their staff seriously and wish to ensure the health and well being of the staff they have working with and for them – some of whom are really struggling with depression and its impact on their total being. Dr Darryl Cross has a style of writing which is readily accessible – a degree in psychology is not required of the reader. What is required is the intent to take an active role in ensuring the health and well being of not only your organisation, but also the staff in that organisation.

Barry J. Fallon, PhD FAPS (Now deceased)
Former Professor of Psychology, School of Psychology,
Australian Catholic University, Fitzroy, Victoria, Australia

Table of Contents

CHAPTER 1

Depression is Expensive

Introduction

For fifteen years, George was a model employee. Loyal, accomplished, energetic, reliable. He was beloved and respected by management and co-workers alike. You could always count on George to come up with that one bright idea that no one else had thought of. He had been around long enough to really know how the organisation worked. You could always count on George to marshal the troops. He always pulled his weight, and then some. He was a team player.

But something has happened to George...

For the past few months, George has been late to work on many days, and when he finally shows up, he is somewhat unkempt, his demeanour is sombre and distracted, and he eats lunch by himself. The dark circles under his eyes suggest that he hasn't had a good night's sleep in weeks – some days it's as if he's sleepwalking through the day. He has called in sick three times in the past six weeks.

In meetings, George pretends to listen, but it's clear that his mind is often somewhere else. He doesn't chime in anymore. More and more, his co-workers are complaining that they have to pick up the slack for him. He forgets to return customer calls. His section of the company's annual report is still unfinished, and the report goes to press today.

No one is quite sure what to say to George. When he enters the room now, conversation fades to awkward silence. If you try to talk to him, he assures you that nothing is wrong, that he's just been "a little blue" lately.

Something has to be done about George…

1.1 The Silent Embezzler

Depression is a common mental disorder around the world although the most modernised and western countries tend to have higher rates of depression.[1,2] According to the World Health Organisation (WHO) in January 2023, more than 280 million people of all ages suffer from depression worldwide.[3] Depression is also a leading cause of disability worldwide and is a primary contributor to the overall global burden of disease.

Depression has a profound impact on health system costs, business productivity and profit, employers and employees, as well as on health, daily functioning, and quality of life for both individuals and families. Depression and suicide are linked, with an estimate that up to 60% of people who commit suicide have major depression.[4]

The National Institute of Mental Health (NIMH) estimates that 19.4 million adults in the **United States of America** had at least one major depressive episode in 2019. This represents 7.8

percent of the US adult population.[5] To illustrate the magnitude of this disorder, consider this: In the US, suicide is the tenth leading cause of death, claiming the lives of more than 47,500 people in 2019. There were almost two and a half times as many suicides as there were homicides (19,141).[6]

On the other side of the globe, **Japan** has one of the highest suicide rates in the world, with more than 30,000 people killing themselves each year since 1998.[7] That number decreased to about 20,000 per year until the coronavirus pandemic (Covid-19) arrived where suicides then increased significantly, especially for women. In October 2020, there was an 83% increase for females compared to the same month the previous year (males suicides rose 22% over the same time period).[8]

In countries like **Australia**, one in every sixteen people is currently experiencing depression, and 6.2% of people aged between 16 to 85 have suffered from depression in the last year. According to the Australian Institute of Health and Welfare, 46% of Australians have experienced a diagnosable mental disorder in their lifetime and 20% in the previous 12 months.[9]

In **Canada** the pattern continues, where 12.2% of the population can expect to experience a depressive disorder in their lifetime, with one in five people experiencing depression in any one year and about 2% of the population depressed at any particular point in time.[10]

Overall, the statistics listed above are **for major depressive disorder only.** When we look at milder depression, it is recognised that symptoms interfere substantially with a person's daily functioning (including work) for 18-52% of people worldwide. These numbers are rising with increasing levels of depression. We are now talking about a significant impact of depression on the workplace, not only in its severe, or clinical form, but also in its milder forms. Moreover, with the coronavirus (Covid-19) completely transforming lives and disrupting every aspect of life as we knew it, mental health concerns, including depression, have been echoed around the globe.

Interestingly, according to the WHO estimates, the **10 most depressed countries in the world** are Ukraine (due no doubt to the war with Russia), followed by the United States, Estonia, Australia, Brazil, Greece, Portugal, Belarus, Finland and Lithuania.[11] On the whole, while Western nations report high levels of subjective well-being, they also report high rates of anxiety and depression. In contrast, Eastern societies appear to be more happy (eg., Solomon Islands, Vanuatu, Laos, Nepal, and the Philippines), and they also experience fewer emotional disorders. Why so? Is this because of under-reporting? Is life perhaps just easier and less stressful? Do Asians and the Pacific Islands perhaps convert psychological disorders into physical symptoms like headaches, stomach aches and insomnia?[12]

Regardless, depression is expensive – for the depressive, for the depressive's family and friends, and for the depressive's employer and co-workers. And we're not just talking about money; it's "expensive" in lots of other ways.

Depression doesn't take time off from work. It trails its victim to the workplace, invading the employee's daily tasks, and insinuating itself into the employee's relationships with colleagues and customers. Depression is skilled at engineering a ripple effect that touches every corner of depressed individuals' lives as well as those around them.

> *"I am now the most miserable man living. If what I feel were equally distributed to the whole human family, there would be not one cheerful face on the earth. Whether I shall ever be better, I cannot tell; I awfully forebode I shall not. To remain as I am is impossible. I must die or be better, it appears to me."*
>
> Abraham Lincoln, 1809-1865
> 16th President of the United States

Depression is disabling. It's that simple. And yet, it is also complicated. Depression is a common illness, so common in fact, that it has been referred to as the "common cold of mental illness". However, far more devastating than the common cold, depression impairs a person's ability to function, both socially and occupationally, and may last a lifetime if left untreated. Repeated plunges into depression lay waste to marriages, families, friendships and careers. And that was before covid-19...

1.2 The Invisible Virus: Coronavirus Pandemic

Although worry, anxiety, and stress are normal human responses to natural and perceived threats, the coronavirus pandemic has heightened people's likelihood of experiencing overwhelming negative emotions like anxiety (and panic) and associated depression.

The fear of contracting this virus was (and is) significant in people's lives as efforts were, and are, being made by governments and authorities around the world to curtail the spread of the virus. Whether the fear has been overplayed by mainstream and social media as well as governments and political leaders has certainly been argued by some.[13,14,15] Regardless, the reality is that the community at large have become very fearful. [16]

It has been reported that on December 31, 2019, Chinese authorities informed the World Health Organisation's China office of pneumonia cases with an apparent unknown cause in Wuhan City, Hubei province. Little did anyone know that the world was about to witness a global pandemic that would shake the existence of humanity to its very foundation (and still is three years after it was first reported and no doubt, will continue to do so in terms of different variants of the original virus).

This virus is considered by many to have escaped from the Wuhan Institute of Virology[17] where "patient zero" was reputedly, a Chinese research scientist.[18,19] Nevertheless, by January 07, 2020, Chinese health authorities announced that the pathogen had been isolated. Covid-19, as it is now called, belongs to the coronavirus family, which also includes Severe Acute Respiratory Syndrome (SARS), Middle East Respiratory Syndrome (MERS), and it spreads through airborne droplets. Meanwhile, as people travelled around China, the virus began spreading outside of the Hubei province. January 9, 2020, was a significant day, albeit negatively, as health officials in China announced the first covid-19 related death. Some time after on March 11, 2020, the World Health Organisation declared the outbreak a global pandemic.[20]

As of mid-June, 2023, more than 767 million people worldwide were reported to have contracted the virus, with over 6.9 million deaths.[21] While the mortality rate is currently much lower than previous pandemics such as the Spanish Flu in 1918-1919 (40-50 million) and HIV/AIDS in 1981 to the present time (25-35 million), the virus's effects have undeniably been felt in all areas of the planet.

In a bid to contain the spread of the virus, economies were shut down worldwide. Schools, religious centres, businesses, community groups, charity groups, churches, retail shops, hotels and cafes, sporting bodies, social clubs, gyms and almost every sector of society were shut down with whole cities and regions locked down. At the same time, people were asked to stay at home, wear masks, physically distance from each other, commit to home schooling, work from home (if possible), and run their businesses and livelihoods from home (if possible). Governments introduced numerous measures to help curb the spread of the virus including digital monitoring like QR codes, vaccine mandates, vaccine passports as well as a host of rules and legislations which curtailed freedoms, and introduced a form of authoritarianism and tyranny including police patrolling, arrests, fines and in some cases imprisonment.

As the coronavirus pandemic swept across the world, a significant degree of fear, concern, worry, and at times overwhelm and panic, were induced in the population at large and was most prevalent in groups such as front-line health workers as well as care providers, older adults, and people who had underlying medical health conditions (eg., diabetes, obesity).

Young adults worldwide, have suffered from coronavirus-related issues because of the closure of educational institutions, interruption to courses or training programs, loss of income or jobs, interruption to their career paths, inability to socialise with their peers, inability to attend parties, birthday celebrations and weddings (and sadly, sometimes funerals), inability to travel and explore the world.

The effects of this pandemic cannot be overestimated. It has had far-reaching consequences more than the spread of the disease itself.

In **sports**, leagues across Europe were suspended or brought to a premature end, causing clubs to lose millions of US dollars in ticket sales and broadcasting revenues. Major sporting events were also cancelled or moved to a future date. The 2020 Summer Olympics and Euro 2020 were most notably postponed to 2021. In the retail sector, demand exceeded supply for most consumables, resulting in empty stores and shelves in supermarkets and shopping centres. Shopping centres around the world reported a shortfall of at least 30%. In the aviation sector, there has been a significant impact. The sector witnessed the cancellation of flights and a massive decline in flight demands by travellers as travel restrictions were put in place. Tourism and hospitality has been decimated.

On April 7, 2020, the International Labour Organisation predicted that there would be a 6.7% loss of job hours globally in the second quarter of 2021. This is the equivalent of 195 million full-time jobs. Also, it was reported that at least 30 million jobs were lost in the first quarter of 2020 alone, greater than the 25 million jobs lost during the financial crisis of 2008.[22]

According to the McKinsey Global Institute in April 2020, it was estimated that covid-19 could cost 57 million people their jobs in the USA with possibly 59 million jobs at risk in the European Union, the UK and Switzerland.[23] In April 2020, more than 20 million Americans were reported to have lost their jobs to that point[24] with unemployment reaching 14.8%, the highest rate since data collection began in 1948.[25]

In Australia, unemployment for persons holding part-time and casual roles increased by a massive 61.2% (eg., hospitality, accommodation, recreation, food services and tourism sectors) especially for the 20-29 year bracket and those over 60 years[26] while in the full-time roles unemployment increased around 3.8%.[27]

The list of the losses goes on and on. *However, what has been consistently omitted from the news is the mental health effects of the virus.* Millions of people have lost their jobs and thousands of businesses already folded; incomes of households have been slashed not to mention careers ruined. Thousands of students who are due to graduate soon will face a tough task securing a job in a coronavirus strained economy. People in their thousands have unexpectedly lost their breadwinners and benefactors to the pandemic.[28]

Some authors have argued that it was the lockdowns, rather than the pandemic itself that impacted lives and mental health. Evidence indicated that a significant number of excess deaths are not due to covid-19, but to drug overdoses, depression and suicide.[15]

Irrespective, depression is an inevitable outcome for people in a pandemic. Many of them have (and will) contemplate suicide. Many who have run into monumental losses or debts may develop severe depression, many students will drop out of education, and many families will struggle to make ends meet.

Thousands of people have given up on their dreams and aspirations. Relationships have been severed; friendships broken; families split apart and fragmented;[29] marriages shattered and cracked. Many now lack the impetus to go on, and many more lack any drive or motivation. All of these factors can lead to depression.

Evidence is consistent that covid-19 has contributed significantly to depression figures internationally. According to the International Organisation for Economic Cooperation and Development (OECD), the prevalence of depression has increased in most countries and, in some cases, even doubled from March 2020. Across various countries, unemployed people and low-income earners have higher rates of depression compared to the rest of the population.[30] According to the medical journal *The Lancet*, covid-19 led to a stark rise in depressive and anxiety disorders globally in 2020; the overall number of cases of mental orders rose dramatically with an additional 53.2 million and 76.2 million cases of anxiety and major depressive disorders respectively.[31,32]

In the **USA**, during the pandemic, about 4 in 10 adults have reported symptoms of anxiety or depressive disorders up from 1 in 10 adults who reported such symptoms from January to June 2019.[33] Furthermore, many adults reported difficulties sleeping (36%) or eating (32%) together with increases in alcohol consumption or substance abuse (12%) as well as worsening chronic conditions (12%) due to worry and stress over the coronavirus. In a further survey conducted June 24-30, 2020, the prevalence of depressive disorder was approximately four times that reported in the second quarter of 2019 (i.e., 24.3% versus 6.5%). Along with this, suicidal ideation was elevated with twice as many respondents reporting serious consideration of suicide in the previous 30 days than did adults in the USA in 2018 (10.7% versus 4.3%).[34]

In the **United Kingdom**, during the early stages of covid, the percentage of people experiencing symptoms of depression and anxiety had risen from 10% to 19% in June 2020.[35]

A **Canadian** survey in early October 2020 found that 22% of Canadians experienced high anxiety levels – four times higher than the pre-pandemic rate – and 13% reported severe depression.[36]

As the pandemic hangs around and the fear also sticks around, the impact to mental health will become much more obvious and apparent.[37]

Initial research on front-line health workers reported in 2000 by Zunin and Myers showed quite clearly that after a pandemic or trauma, there is a prolonged period that goes well beyond the initial event or crisis. Once the crisis is over, people struggle over a prolonged period of time and for at least a year or more.[38] The case is made here though, that in a sense, **all of the population in every country has been "front-line"** and as such, the exhaustion, burn-out and ultimately, depression, will linger (and maybe for years to come as people struggle to get back on their feet again – and some never will).

Given that the pandemic has been enduring and given that repeated lockdowns have occurred in some countries like Australia (the State of Victoria and Melbourne, its capital, had the world's longest lockdown), there is and will be, a prolonged period of depression for many. Sadly though, after repeated lockdowns with government restrictions, freedoms taken away, enforcement and digital monitoring, many may simply have given up with what psychologists call "learned helplessness".[39]

Nevertheless, these people will try to find work and some will end up in work... but depressed.

1.3 The Silent Embezzler in the Workplace

Since depression often goes undiagnosed, statistics vary on its occurrence in the workplace. The general consensus of national and world health organisations is that 1 in 6.8 people (14.7%) will suffer from some form of mental health issue while on the job. What this suggests is that on any given day, around 15% of your organisation's employees are struggling mentally and may be clinically depressed.[40]

You are probably aware that depression is widespread, but what you may not know is that it has become one of industry's most expensive illnesses.

Depression was a global economic problem even before covid-19, and it impacts practically every company in the world. It is a leading cause of diminished productivity in the workforce due to **absenteeism** (in the UK it is estimated that 12.7% of all sickness absence days are attributable to mental health issues)[40] and **presenteeism**, i.e., workers who come to work and are on the job, but because of medical conditions such as depression, are not fully functioning or fully present, causing their work performance and productivity to suffer.

How dramatically does depression impact the workplace? Consider these startling global statistics:

- Worldwide, 17-21% of the general workforce experiences short-term disability during any given year.

- 37-48% of workers suffering from depression experience short-term disability during any given year.[41]

- Depression and anxiety are the most common workplace problems needing the attention of employee assistance professionals. [42]

- The number of workdays lost each year due to depression are as follows:

    U.S.:   200 million[43]
    Australia: 8 million[44]
    U.K.:   70 million[45]
    Canada: Every week at least 500,000 Canadians miss work due to mental illness[46]

What does this mean in terms of financial burden? What does it mean in relation to lost productivity? Look at these staggering statistics for lost productivity from clinical depression:

    U.S.: $51 billion(US) per year in absenteeism and $26 billion in treatment costs[47]
    Australia: $5.3 billion(AU) per year[44]
    Canada: $51 billion(CAN) per year for mental illness[48]
    U.K.:   £2.4 million per year[49]

Recent data for example, for 2020, from the United States shows the following:

- Depression interferes with a person's ability to complete physical job tasks about 20% of the time and reduces cognitive performance about 35% of the time.

- Only 57% of employees who report moderate depression and 40% of those who report severe depression receive treatment to control depression symptoms.

- In addition to absenteeism, depression accounts for more than 12 million days of reduced productivity each year.

- Between 1.8% and 3.6% of workers in the US labour force suffer from major depression.

- According to one survey, 88% of workers (participants) experienced at least one symptom of depression during the coronavirus pandemic; 52% lost interest in doing things; 52% had trouble sleeping; 51% felt hopeless; one out of six started therapy for the first time in 2020 due to the pandemic; and 15% increased medication dosage.[50]

The statistics above show that while we have a medical pandemic on our hands, we also have **workplace depression which is considered an epidemic, and it's not going away either**. It's a pervasive human condition that will continue to plague business as long as we continue to employ humans to conduct business. Yet more than 50% of individuals who suffer from clinical depression never receive treatment. In fact, the World Health Organisation states that less than 25% of those affected receive treatment and that in some countries, it is less than 10%.

Who's to blame? Who's responsibility is this? Depressed workers, who are in denial or don't seek help or managers who are ignorant about the situation or who don't step in to offer assistance? Does management have a responsibility to provide support and treatment for depressed workers? More people have reportedly developed depression due to the coronavirus pandemic, so where should responsibility be apportioned?

Employee disability, after all, has legal ramifications for organisations. Should managers intervene when they observe signs of what they think might be depression in an employee? Do they have the right to screen for depressive tendencies during hiring and recruiting?

This book seeks to answer these questions. It explores practical, effective intervention strategies, and discusses the legal implications of taking a proactive approach to managing depression in the workplace.

1.4 A Series of Catch-22s

Depression wreaks havoc with what makes us most human – our self-esteem and self-confidence, our communication, our attitudes, our relationships, and our ability to trust our own judgment about those closest to us. We have a basic human instinct to help the 'Georges' in our companies – as managers, as co-workers, and as friends.

But what does "help" mean? Extending that helping hand is not without its complications or its issues.

Sometimes depressed employees don't realise they're depressed or are oblivious to the impact of their illness on productivity – their own, and that of the co-workers who must compensate for their impaired performance. We must also consider the unfortunate stigma that society has stamped on psychological disorders. Often, depressives are ostracised by co-workers, which provides yet more evidence to the depressed individual of their personal defects, fuelling a cycle of guilt and shame, hopelessness and worthlessness – a vicious, recurring cycle of depression.

It's no wonder that many depressives deny, avoid, marginalise or rationalise their symptoms, and often never acknowledge or discuss them. Depressed individuals are almost invariably concerned about confidentiality, fearful that acknowledgment will cost them their job. They're afraid to seek treatment, worried about the cost and whether their health insurance will cover it. A particularly cruel twist of irony is that their general lack of motivation, which is a common symptom of depression, contributes to preventing them from asking for help.

Depression impacts the workplace in subtle, incalculable ways. Employee morale, after all, can be tricky to measure, often quantifiable only when productivity is so severely diminished that the company's bottom line has been dramatically affected or teamwork and relationships significantly impacted.

How many good employees are you losing to depression? You may be losing people who, with proper treatment, would recover quickly and become model employees again. Perhaps some of your best workers are leaving your company because they've grown tired of enduring a depressed co-worker day in and day out. Others might leave because they resent having to compensate for the depressed co-worker's impaired job performance.

"When my marriage fell over, I was devastated. But true to form, I knew that I had to soldier on. It's just what you do. Thankfully, we didn't have any kids. I continued to work, but in retrospect, I know that I wasn't performing all that well. I felt kind of unreal the whole time. It was almost like I was watching myself in a stage play or theatre performance. I felt detached from myself and just sort of went through the motions. I almost felt numb.

I was sitting in my car in the parking lot one day with my head slumped against the steering wheel and my boss saw me and came over to me. In hindsight, that was the best thing that could have happened because it spurred me to go and get help.

My boss was very supportive and said that he'd noticed that I had lapses in concentration and really hadn't been myself since the relationship breakdown."

1.5 The Cost of Depression to Your Company

The costs of absenteeism, presenteeism and low productivity vary widely from industry to industry and company to company. However, there are both **direct** and **indirect** costs.

1.5.1 Direct Costs

Economic theory holds that the value of an employee's output should be at least equal to the employee's compensation, including wages and benefits. What the employee puts in in terms of time and energy is compensated for in terms of salary and benefits. So, unless the workload is redistributed to other employees, the output loss equals their compensation for the absence period.

In the U.S., employers offer health care benefits as part of compensation packages in order to attract and retain good employees.[51] But as health care costs rise, insurance rates rise as well, so the employer eventually will pay more for depressed employees, who cost more than 2.5 times as much in prescription medications as employees without depression, and who require nearly three times as many prescriptions per year.

Interestingly, it has been concluded that depressed patients in the U.S. were as functionally impaired (in terms of physical, social, and role functioning) as those with medical disorders such as hypertension, diabetes, advanced coronary artery disease, back problems, angina, arthritis, breathing problems, and gastro-intestinal disorders.[52] It's not unreasonable to suggest that this would be similar in other Western style countries like Australia.

Furthermore, depression is linked to chronic conditions such as anxiety disorders, sleep disorders, stomach hyperactivity, elevated cholesterol, hypertension, inflammatory conditions and asthma.[53] Increased absences for these additional conditions, therefore, can also be linked to depression.

For countries outside the U.S., direct costs are in relation to hiring employee assistance providers, costs associated with *WorkCover* claims in which depression is shown to have been caused by the work setting, costs associated with the hiring of nursing or medical staff, and the costs of absenteeism as discussed above. In countries such as Australia and the U.K., employees fund their own private health care as well as relying on relatively effective public health systems (which incidentally are currently overburdened). However, it is the indirect costs that employers generally overlook and of which, they need to be more aware.

1.5.2 Indirect Costs

As an indicator of what indirect costs might look like, studies in the US for example have tried to quantify what this could be. The indirect costs of depression, including mortality, may be seven times as burdensome as the direct medical costs.[54] In a survey conducted by the University of Michigan Depression

Center in 2004, managers believed that depression was the leading inhibitor of worker productivity. About 78% of health benefit managers believe that lost productivity and absenteeism actually cost the company more than does treating their depressed workers.[55]

Hidden depression in the workplace leads to absenteeism, diminished productivity, job dissatisfaction, substance abuse and accidents. In fact, it has been shown that depressed workers lost 1.5 to 3.2 more days due to absenteeism than other workers in a thirty-day period.[56] Employees with depression reported an average of 5.6 hours per week lost productive time, whereas those without depression lost only 1.5 hours of productive time.

Extrapolation of these data suggests that workers with depression in the U.S. cost employers an estimated $44 billion per year in lost productivity – $31 billion per year more than non-depressed workers.

Added to these hidden or indirect costs are those resulting from impacts on the work of other employees, such as:

- Disrupted workflow

- Extra supervisory time required

- Overtime pay for employees who must compensate for absenteeism or lowered productivity on the part of the depressed worker

- Training costs for employees to be skilled-up to undertake the tasks of the depressed worker

- Negative morale

For your company, there may be even **further** specific cost factors to evaluate. For example:

- **Skill level of the absent employee.** Absences of employees with specific, refined skills are more costly, as is replacement training for those particular positions.

- **Wage of the absent employee.** Absences of employees with higher wages are generally more costly than absences of lower-wage employees.

- **The nature of the production process.** Some labour is essential to earning revenue, i.e., the labour can be directly tied to daily business operations. Other labour may be nonessential, i.e., the business will continue to operate and earn revenue without it, even if not as effectively.

- **How the absentee process is managed by your organisation.** Some methods of dealing with absenteeism are more costly than others. For example, hiring replacement workers may be more expensive than retraining existing workers.

1.5.3 The Depression Calculator

In conjunction with Pharmaceutical Research and Manufacturers of America (PhRMA) and others, the American Psychiatric Association developed a Productivity Impact Model which is also known as the Depression Calculator (http://www.depressioncalculator.com).

This tool enables employers to view what effect improved treatment of depression could have on their bottom line. The program examines a company's workforce by age, estimates how many employees in each age group are likely to be affected, and projects savings based on reduced absenteeism and reduced direct medical costs.

Evaluating the impact of depression on productivity starts with four simple assumptions:

1. **Employees affected by depression miss work more frequently.** Estimates vary widely, but we will use a conservative range of 22 to 32 workdays missed per year, including both absenteeism and presenteeism.

2. **Employees affected by depression incur higher medical costs.** A conservative range is a $1,000 to $2,000 increase in medical costs per depressed worker per year. Research also indicates that depressed workers are less compliant with treatment regimens for other co-existing medical conditions, and are more likely to engage in high-risk behaviours linked to other health conditions and accidents.

3. **It costs companies money when workers miss work due to depression.** It costs additional money to hire and train replacement workers and/or additional workers to cover lost productivity caused by depressed workers' absenteeism and presenteeism.

4. **Absenteeism rates and medical costs can be reduced when depression is successfully treated.** The Productivity Impact Model assumes a 77% reduction in absenteeism/presenteeism under what is called "enhanced care", and a 51% reduction under what is termed "usual care", though some studies show as much as a 70% reduction in

absenteeism under usual care.

[**Note: "Usual care"** for depression is the level of care that patients generally receive in primary care settings such as the general practitioner's office. Research indicates, though, that doctors generally under-detect and under-manage the condition.
"Enhanced care" for depression is a collaborative care model in which a care manager (e.g., a nurse, psychologist, or social worker) educates the patient about evidence-based treatment for the disorder, encourages them to initiate and comply with this treatment, proactively monitors their treatment response over time, cues providers to changes, and adjusts treatment for patients who are failing to respond.]

Now let's take a look at some hard numbers.

Let's say your company has 1,000 employees. Using the PhRMA Productivity Impact Model, we can conservatively estimate that 66 (6.6%) of those employees are affected by clinical depression during a given twelve-month period.

Taking the calculations further, we get:

	Minimum	Maximum
Number of missed workdays per affected employee	22	32
Additional direct medical costs per employee	$1,000	$2,000
Total workdays missed for affected employees	1,449	2,106

Estimated replacement costs for absenteeism (based on an average daily wage of $147.50 per worker – $173 for men, $122 for women – an 80% replacement rate)	$237,168	$344,986
Estimated incremental medical costs	$65,820	$131,639
Total costs	**$302,988**	**$476,625**

So 66 depressed workers could cost your company **$302,988 to $476,625 per year.** Even without incremental medical costs that the company may not incur, **the cost is still estimated to be between $237,168 and $344,986.** Remember too, we were being conservative with our figures, as explained above.

The U.S. communications giant Sprint decided to launch an initiative in relation to depression within its workforce and ran the model in order to understand the costs of the disease and the potential savings it could realise by improving treatment. The company also looked at how much it was spending on pharmaceuticals for its depressed work staff. Based on their findings, they decided to roll out a depression awareness and education program that was financially very successful. Interestingly, employers are also realising that depression is an area in which they can make a positive difference in people's lives.

1.6 Is There a Solution?

More than 70% of people diagnosed with depression are employed.[57] While this statistic relates to the U.S. workforce, it is suggested that it may not be too different in other westernised countries such as Australia, Canada, and the U.K., as well as other European countries. Overwhelmingly, employees who reported staying home from work or having difficulty completing their work because of depression felt that their performance improved after receiving treatment.

Most people who suffer from depression need treatment to get better. It's difficult to pull yourself up by your own bootstraps.

Medical advances have given us effective new medications, psychotherapies and alternative natural treatments for treating workers with this disabling disorder.

The good news?

About 80% of those who suffer from clinical depression can be successfully treated, feel better and show markedly improved performance within a few short weeks. With early diagnosis, intervention and support, most people can conquer clinical depression and resume normal social and occupational functioning. Organised screening and enhanced depression treatment can significantly improve outcomes for depressed workers, *and* for the companies that employ them.

Research by PhRMA, however, indicates that up to 50% of employees suffering from clinical depression are undiagnosed and go untreated (the World Health Organisation indicates that less than 25% are treated). Historically, employers haven't evaluated the true costs of untreated depression, particularly the indirect costs. Further complicating matters, the workers' compensation system and the courts have been slow to recognise depression as a work-related disability.

Today, 40-60% of U.S. worksites with more than fifty employees offer some type of mental health program, including stress management programs and Employee Assistance Programs (EAPs).[58] This figure is replicated in other parts of the world where EAPs have been accepted as a necessary adjunct to the companies' cultures and to human resources programs.

Among other things, employers have a clear financial incentive to identify and treat employees who suffer from depression. Investing in healthy human capital pays large dividends in the long run. Companies that invest in their workforces today will emerge as productivity leaders tomorrow.

For example, the Australian Health and Performance Study results showed a clear association between employee health status and performance. Firms such as Oracle, Vodafone, Integral Australia and Unisys Australia have been quick to embrace new evaluation tools to measure the bottom-line impact of wellness programs. Results from an on-line survey by Unisys Australia found that the firm was losing 27,593 workdays through the poor health of its employees (including depressed persons). Therefore, Unisys implemented a 12-month program for employees encompassing a hydration campaign, a physical activity education and interactive team challenge, a nutrition program, and a strength and resilience program which concentrated on stress management.

A reassessment of employees at the end of the 12 months showed an average 5.7% overall improvement in health and well-being. Areas recording particularly strong improvement included stress (11%), risk behaviour (8.8%), and nutrition (4.2%). Importantly, Unisys calculated that the financial savings to the business exceeded $4.9 million, achieving the organisation a return on investment of $4.13 for every $1 invested in reduced absenteeism, and $17.50 for every $1 invested in improving effectiveness.

Although mental health services were already over-stretched before the coronavirus pandemic, the scale of depression since the start of the pandemic meant that an unprecedented level of mental health support is required to prevent permanent mental damage.

Several countries have taken instant steps to increase mental health support, with new mental health information and phone support lines giving tips on coping and prevention methods during the coronavirus pandemic. Many countries also increased entitlements to mental health services and mental health funding.

Measures were also put in place by several countries to protect jobs and incomes (such as job retention schemes), and to aid an easy transition to working from home.

The Dark Clouds at Work: Depression in the Workplace and What to do About it will increase your understanding of depression and the true costs of depression in the workplace, give you the tools to effectively manage depression in your workplace and, ultimately, promote a more favourable environment orientated towards resilience and recovery.

Chapter 1 Summary

Depression is a world-wide phenomenon although largely restricted to more Western societies.

However, the coronavirus has had a massive effect on depression (which may also mean that depression could now be experienced more readily in Eastern societies as well). During the heat of the pandemic, four out of ten adults in the US reported symptoms of depression. The rate of depressive symptoms also increased from 14.6% to 48.3% in the general population.

Consider the statistics. In the U.S., for example, about 16.2 million people have experienced a major depressive disorder at some time in their lives; in Canada, 12.2% of people are expected to have a major depressive disorder over the course of their lives, and in Australia, 6.2% of its population are expected to.

The general consensus of national and world health organisations is that on any given day, between 3.6% and 9% of your organisation's employees are clinically depressed. However, that doesn't account for the other 18-52% of people who are mildly depressed and are at work, but are not fully functioning or not performing at their optimal level. **Not surprisingly, depression is a leading cause of diminished productivity in the workforce due to absenteeism and presenteeism.**

There are substantial direct and indirect costs to businesses resulting from depressed workers. It has been estimated that depression costs the U.S. $51.5 billion(US) a year in lost productivity, Australia $5.3 billion(AU) a year, and the U.K. £2.4 billion a year.

It has been estimated that in Australia alone, each full-time employee with untreated clinical depression costs an organisation $9,665 per year.

We cannot escape this ensuing crisis enveloping our lives and our workplaces, or its associated economic impacts. Neither can the wider impact of the coronavirus on our lives (e.g., lockdowns, restrictions and the fear generated by the media), be underestimated and that impact does not seem to be going away. It's called depression.

"It's a recession when your neighbour loses his job; it's a depression when you lose yours."

Harry S Truman, 1884-1972
33rd President of the United States

CHAPTER 2

Workplace Depression Is On The Rise

Introduction

Certainly, workplace depression has always existed. With the global financial crisis in 2008 however, depression levels rose to new highs and then with the covid-19 pandemic, depression figures rose significantly again.

Note this report from CNN dated 28 January, 2009:
Amber Easton has gone from $80,000 a year in salary to scrambling for work. At a time in her life when she should be scaling the corporate ladder, she has instead spiralled into a deep depression. She recently lost her car and now faces eviction from her apartment.

Just last week, the 35-year-old long-time working professional attended two job fairs with friends in the Detroit area. They stood in line for over three hours with hundreds of professionals of all types.

"It was a real eye-opener to see the calibre of people we were in line with – very educated with vast skill sets," Easton said in an e-mail. "Afterwards, we went to the restaurant located in the same hotel and it was filled with unemployed professionals sharing their story, from engineers to graphic designers to marketing professionals."

Easton's saga began in July 2007 when she traded in her job as a corporate compliance officer to attend law school, what she thought would help advance her career. But after a year of law school, she decided it wasn't for her. By then, her old job was gone and the job market had shrunk.

"It's hard not to be depressed during a time like this," she said. "I never imagined in a million years that I would be in such a situation at my age and at this point in my career. I am humiliated. I am praying for everyone else out there who is facing the same problems."

She has applied to 70 different companies but gotten few leads. She recently went through a rigorous interview process for one job in another state, but to no avail.

Every day, she searches for new job possibilities and every day results in more desperation. She estimates she's making $20,000 – "if that" – as a contract employee working from her home. "I just haven't made enough to keep up."

Prior to the current economic woes, for many employers, escalating disability claims and diminished productivity left no doubt that the incidence of depression in the workplace was increasing. Since covid-19, any employers still in doubt have had those doubts annihilated with employees, managers and leaders feeling exhausted leading to burnout and frequently depression.[1]

Medical research backs up the increased rates of depression. There had been a significant rise in the number and rate of outpatients being treated for depression over the last twenty-five years. In 1987, 0.73 per 100 persons were treated on an outpatient basis for depression. By 1997, that rate had increased to 2.33 per 100 persons. That's an increase of 300%.[2] Why? After all, don't we have better research, more knowledge and more effective treatments now than ever before?

Workplace studies suggest that workers can provide the answers, if employers are willing to listen. Even back in 2004, a survey by the American Psychological Association (APA),[2] for example, revealed the following:

- One in four workers took a mental health day off from work to cope with stress.

- 62% of Americans said work was the number one cause of stress in their lives.

- 54% of workers were concerned about health problems caused by stress.

Increased stress tends to drive people toward unhealthy stress management behaviours (that further fuel depression), such as smoking, comfort eating, poor diet choices, inactivity and drinking alcohol. Dependence on unhealthy behaviours leads to serious long-term health problems and, of course, even deeper depression.

Irrespective of where the world is ending up as a result of the pandemic, depression was already steadily increasing prior to 2020. The bottom line though for employers is higher HR costs (e.g., Employee Assistance Programs, hiring and training new recruits) and unhealthy, unhappy, unproductive employees which of course, impacts the profit and loss sheet.

2.1 The Great Resignation

As Covid-19 continued, by the end of 2020, it became clear that burnout and exhaustion were the by-products for workers and not just those at the front-line.[1] As a New York Times article in April 2021 reported, based on a study of 2,651 employees conducted by MetLife, *"Malaise, burnout, depression and stress are all up considerably"*.

Workers in 2020 experienced a range of emotions from initial concern to acute anxiety and sometimes panic. There were periods of confusion, uncertainty and at times desperation. At times, employees felt angry and betrayed. Some leaders have told the author that initially they were in shock and they felt numb, unable to make a decision or know what to do. Many just wanted to give up; it was just too hard. Many leaders, managers and employees didn't think that they would make it through, and unfortunately, some didn't, and their businesses collapsed (and some are still collapsing).

Both leaders and workers alike reported to the author comments such as:

"There's nothing left in the tank"
"I feel tired all the time and I can't work out what's wrong with me"

> *"My batteries are flat"*
> *"I'm cooked"*
> *"I don't really want to come to work now"*
> *"I'm dragging myself around here"*
> *"I'm not up for it anymore... I'm toast"*
> *"All the managers are feeling the same... we're all done"*
> *"I'm not sure what's wrong with me... I'm usually up and about after a Christmas break"*
> *"I feel tired by 11am and done by lunchtime"*

Towards the end of 2021, with continued outbreaks of different variants, continued lockdowns including schools and businesses, vaccine mandates being imposed, freedoms being restricted or cut-off, digital monitoring still occurring, and vaccine passports being introduced, the burnout turned to despair and a sense of hopelessness and at times anger, aggression and violence. When will this ever end? I can't take much more! Will it ever be over? People had had enough.

Not surprisingly, the "great resignation" started to unfold. Towards the end of 2021, the trend of people leaving the workplace revealed itself. The signs had been coming and were there, but employees started to vote with their feet and move to the exit door. This is a world-wide trend. A survey of 25 countries by HR technology company, The Adecco Group, found Australian workers however, were the most burnt-out through the world with about 50% having to take leave for their mental health. Not surprising really given that as Reuters News Service reported on 21 October, 2021 *"Melbourne readies to exit world's longest COVID-19 lockdown"*.

Sadly, the only discussion re lockdowns in Australia was about a sole focus on health. **No consideration was given to**

the rest of life; to economic devastation, loss of businesses, unemployment, careers and livelihoods destroyed, education halted or disrupted, not to mention the toll on families, marriages, relationships, friendships and of course, the impact on mental health.

Harvard Business Review found that employees between 30-45 years had the greatest increase in resignations rates with both tech and healthcare industries being the highest areas for resignations.[4]

Why the resignations?

Basically it comes down to this, how staff were treated over the past couple of years during covid.

Those who stayed put were from companies where support, understanding and open communication were in place. Simple really. What was needed was some common sense related to care and support. Sadly, numbers of leaders and executive teams don't have this crucial ingredient. It's called empathy and it's called emotional intelligence. They are paying for it in resignations.[4]

2.2 Depression Among Occupations

Depression is no respecter of persons in the same way that depression is no respecter of industries or professions.

Back in 2007, findings from a survey of 7,500 professionals in Australia showed higher than average levels of depressive symptoms when compared to the general Australian population.[5] The results are reflected below in Table 2.1.

Table 2.1

Profession	% *
Accounting	10
Consulting	7
Engineering	8
Law	16
Patent Attorney	13
Actuarial Firm	8
IT Services	10
Architectural	9
Insurance Underwriting	10
Insurance Brokering	6

(* % with moderate or severe depressive symptoms)

The statistics show that individuals from the legal professions were more likely to report moderate to severe symptoms of depression when compared to the total sample. Around 16% of legal professionals experienced moderate or severe depressive symptoms, a rate 2.5 times that of the general population.

The next group of professions is patent attorneys, accountants, insurance underwriters, and IT services, were most likely to suffer depression where people in these jobs had a 10% chance or greater of suffering depressive symptoms while the average for the general population was 6.34%. These kinds of careers are generally under pressure with deadlines for clients, are often dealing with crises or urgent matters, and they are usually high achievers and have worked hard to get where they are. They can also be hard on themselves and feel the pressure of pleasing clients as well as not losing any clients. All of these factors can contribute to the risk of depression.

Furthermore, a significant proportion of those surveyed openly reported that they used alcohol and non-prescription drugs to manage their feelings of sadness and depression. In relation to the professions, it was lawyers and members of actuarial firms who had the highest alcohol and drug use, followed by insurance underwriters and architects.

Jonathon sat across from me looking down at the table. He was 44 years of age and a highly successful lawyer. He had been with his firm for fifteen years and had been a partner for nine years.

He seemed depressed, and further conversation revealed that he could have been diagnosed as clinically depressed.

He said that he was "burnt-out". He didn't like what this job had changed him into. He didn't like the way that his personality had changed in that he wasn't the same kind of guy that he was when he first started in his career. He felt alienated from his family and had lost contact with his children. He'd had enough.

He had thought long and hard about his future over the previous twelve months and now had decided to move back to working three days a week with a goal of leaving the firm altogether in about 12-18 months. He said that he knew his other law partners would be upset with him, and some would think that he'd "lost his marbles", but he knew what he had to do.

He wasn't concerned about the fact that his salary would drop significantly. It just wasn't worth it, he said. "I need to find myself again…and I need to re-connect with my wife and kids again. I need to live again."

He therefore wanted to start the process of coaching with me in regards to finding some happiness and fulfillment, as well as finding a new career path.

More recently, a study of occupations within the USA, listed the top 10 jobs with the highest rates of depression.[6] Understandably, different kinds of careers can create different tensions and stressors especially if physical safety is threatened or if the job involves dealing with trauma or crises such as front-line responders (e.g., police, paramedics, firemen). The list below is therefore interesting and not what one might typically expect:

- Public and Private Transportation (16.2%)
- Real Estate (15.7%)
- Social Services (14.6%)
- Manufacturing or Production (14.3%)
- Personal Services (14.3%)
- Legal Services (13.4%)
- Environmental and Waste Services (13.4%)
- Organisation and Association Administration (13.3%)
- Security and Commodities Broker (12.6%)
- Print and Publishing (12.4%)

However, a recent study released in October 2020 by Monash University in Melbourne, Australia, identified occupations with a greater risk of suicide.[7] This study reviewed more than 60 international studies for the prevalence for suicide death, ideation and attempts. Results showed the following:

- **Farming and Agriculture:** People in this category have more access to lethal means. Anecdotally, the fact that the job is 24-7 and you never really switch off as well as having to cope at times, with harsh and variable weather conditions (as well as market variability) can take its toll.

- **Veterinarians:** The suicide rate amongst vets is twice as high than in other health disciplines and four times higher than in the general population with again, access to lethal means with 80% of cases in Australia involving self-poisoning with a drug used to euthanasia animals. Again, anecdotally, this kind of career is 24-7 and vets receive a good deal of abuse and aggression from pet owners over costs (pet bills are straight out of an owner's pocket since there is no reimbursement from anywhere) as well as unrealistic expectations from owners regarding their pets' health, rehab or recovery.

- **Medical Practitioners:** Female doctors are more likely to suicide than males with self-poisoning again the most common lethal means. Relationship problems were the most frequently cited life events prior to the suicides for both groups.

- **Nursing and Midwifery:** Suicide risk is higher for nurses and midwives than those in other occupations.

- **Paramedics:** There is a lack of data on this group except that anecdotally, being at the front-line for trauma can cause burnout and Post-traumatic Stress Disorder (PTSD).

- **Firefighters:** Again, there is a lack of data on suicide risk for this group except that as before, burnout and PTSD is common.

- **Law Enforcement:** While international data shows an increased risk of suicide among police and correctional officers (suicide up to 69% higher than the general population), that trend is not reflected in Australia for police officers. However, there is an increased risk for correctional officers.

- **Construction:** Those in lower-skilled roles in Australian construction such as machinists and labourers showed double the suicide risk in comparison to other occupations.

- **Creative Industries:** UK studies showed that artists, musicians, actors, entertainers and media presenters have a higher risk of suicide than the general population while, in Australia, for the entertainment industry, suicidal thoughts were six times higher than the general population, with four times greater for planning, and twice as likely to attempt suicide.

There is no single explanation for depression's escalation in the workplace or across professions, but we know some of the reasons for it, although the unprecedented impact of covid-19 has significantly increased the prevalence and incidence of mental health issues. Addressing these issues is a very necessary and critical place to start.

2.3 Reason 1: Stress Levels Have Increased

In recent years, much research has been devoted to the impact of stress on depression. Evidence suggests that we are not just getting soft in our lifestyles – quite the opposite. The stress of modern life is increasing at an alarming rate: 45% over the last thirty years, according to some surveys.[8]

Most of us are simply living more stressful lives. One of the prime reasons is the introduction of technology into our lives especially the mobile phone and mobile devices like the tablet or i-pad. We are now on 24-7. Some executives have confided that even when they are on holidays, they constantly check their emails. Every day we find ourselves juggling work, family, and community obligations, and often – let's face it – not well.

One third of Americans admit having trouble balancing their work and family lives.[3] We're certainly living busier, more competitive lives, made even more competitive, occupationally speaking, by an increasingly competitive global economy (although since covid there has been a trend away from international suppliers and customers to being more sovereign and national). The U.S. Occupational Safety and Health Administration, however, has actually gone so far as to declare stress "a hazard of the workplace".

Believe it or not, people are choosing to work rather than take annual leave. Australians have about 123 million days of accrued leave valued at $33.3 billion and that was back in 2008! Nearly 60% of full-time workers do not use their full 4 weeks annual leave each year and have accrued 8 weeks or more according to a survey by Tourism Australia.[9] It's not hard to imagine why we are feeling more stressed when we don't take legitimate breaks and we keep working.

The same is true of every westernized country, especially now that the world has experienced an unprecedented pandemic followed by an economic downturn globally. We have to do more with less. Back in 2008, a survey conducted by the

American Psychological Society showed that 80% of Americans were stressed about the economy. The "Boomers" (44-62 years) and "Builders" or "Matures" (63+ years) were more stressed than were the "Gen X" (30-43 years) and "Gen Y" (18-29 years); 85% versus 74% respectively.[7]

More recently, Moss in her 2021 book titled, *"The Burnout Epidemic"* reports that in a survey of 50,000 participants, it was evident that scores on the scales of exhaustion and cynicism had both risen significantly.[11] Exhaustion because people are working hard to keep their work and personal lives afloat along with more than two years of a pandemic including lockdowns, restrictions of personal freedoms, border closures and upheavals. Cynicism because of a lack of trust in the world. As Moss comments, *"So many people feel let down by their government's poor preparation for the pandemic, as well as by the injustices in work and well-being that the pandemic has highlighted"* (p.10).

2.4 Reason 2: Workplace Stress Has Increased

Stress in the workplace is a growing concern for employees and employers in various countries, including Australia. Figures show that while workers' compensation claims made by Australian employees fell significantly between 1996 and 2004, the number of stress-related claims almost doubled. Further, **workplace stress** is costing the Australian economy $14.81 billion (AU) per year. Stress-related presenteeism and absenteeism are directly costing Australian employers $10.11 billion a year. About 3.2 days per worker are lost each year due to workplace stress.

Typically, both Europe and the U.K. top the list of European countries for long hours, where the UK is the only country that allows staff to opt out of the forty-eight hour per work week limit introduced across the European Union as a health and safety measure. It is reported that "Britain's long-hours culture is a national disgrace. It leads to stress, ill-health and family strains". This is a long-term trend. A paper published back in the early 2000s in the British Journal of Industrial Relations highlighted that work effort had intensified over the previous two decades.[12]

The workplace is a site of changing demographics too. With flexible schedules, two working-parent families, working mums, and adults caring for elderly parents – not to mention the stress that technologies such as mobile or cell phones, smart phones, i-phones, and video-conferencing introduce to workers' time and privacy – stress brings a new face to the working adult today.

Not surprisingly, according to authors Joel Gosh, Jeffrey Pfeffer, and Stefanos Zenios, work is the fifth leading cause of death in the United States, a statistic made famous in Prefers' book titled, *"Dying for a Paycheck".*[13] The International Labour Organisation reports that excessively long working hours contribute to the deaths of 2.8 million workers every year. Further, work-related pressure has increased over the past five years with more than one-third of respondents citing excessive work and tight deadlines as their major concerns.[14]

Then a crisis like a pandemic hits world-wide and significantly escalates an already severe problem.

What is it that has caused stress to also increase at the coal-face, so to speak? Anecdotally, there is good evidence to suggest that it has, but let's look more closely at why.

2.4.1 Insufficient Wages

Back in 2008, about 81% of Americans named **money** as the number one factor that affects their stress level. It's probably true that we'd all like more in the pay packet, but clearly, it is an issue for a sizeable majority.[10] Fast forward to 2018, and money is still the biggest source of stress. According to a study conducted by the American Psychological Association, *"Regardless of the economic climate, money and finances have remained the top stressor since our survey began in 2007".*[15]

2.4.2 Increased Demands

Approximately 61% of U.S. workers list **heavy workloads** as a significant impact on work stress levels – in other words, having too much to do and too little time to do it, too many demands, not enough resources or staff, gruelling deadlines, unreasonable time demands, shift work, too much responsibility, and having to make frequent on-the-spot decisions. It's called work overwhelm and work overload. Anecdotally, this is what the Australian, Irish and Canadian workforce complains about too.

One study of 200 women in Sweden revealed that increased cortisol showed up in the saliva of women when they overworked. An overabundance of cortisol can cause hypertension, immune deficiency, and unsustainable weight gain. Further participants with excessive overtime (more than 10 hours per week) had on average, cortisol levels about twice as high as women with moderate overtime (less than 10 hours per week).[16]

Another study by the University College London of over 600,000 workers found that those who worked more than 55 hours per week had a 13% greater risk of a heart attack and were 33% more likely to suffer a stroke compared to those who worked 35-40 hours per week.[17]

The advent of technology colliding with a pandemic meant that there was an even greater tendency for workers to be "always on". There is no real down time. According to the National Bureau of Economic Research, the number of meetings has increased by 12.9%; data from North America, Europe, and the Middle East shows the workday added exactly 48.5 minutes which is almost a 9% increase between 2019 and 2020.[18]

Additionally, data from NordVPN shows that employees are logging three hours more per day on the job than before city and state-wide covid lockdowns. Another VPN provider, Surfshark, revealed spikes in usage showed up between midnight and 3.00am which were not present before 2020.[19] Because of having to work from home, the boundaries between home and work have virtually disappeared. People are simply not escaping work. There's simply no-where to go and there was no commute time to both wind up to the day and wind down from the day.

Further personal research over the last thirty years has shown the author that added to work overload are the following factors creating work stress:

- **conflict with clients** (customers are very demanding and criticise staff or even verbally abuse them (and occasionally physically assault them); this has escalated since covid-19, with customer abuse regarding legislated or policy restrictions and limitations that in many ways do not make sense)

- **changes in the job** (restructuring, changes in policy and procedures, altered job duties, demotion, over-promotion, lack of adequate preparation, lack of training, excessive job rotation; needless to say, job changes have also escalated during the pandemic)

- **role conflict and ambiguity** (being given different instructions by different supervisors, not knowing exactly what you have to do or when or where, unclear job requirements)

- **inadequate support from supervisors** (feeling unappreciated or misunderstood, lack of recognition from the boss, a boss who is quick to criticise, but not to encourage, unrealistic expectations; support from bosses was considered paramount during the pandemic, but sadly, many leaders either did not know how to show empathy or provide support or they were overwhelmed themselves)

2.4.3 Job Insecurity

Originally, around 45% of workers in the U.S. said job insecurity had a significant impact on work stress levels. Many workers felt less secure about their careers as a result of higher turnover rates and economic upheavals that led to bankruptcies, downsizing, layoffs and mergers.

This uncertainty increased after the world economic crisis and downturn in 2008 which resulted in numerous countries announcing that they were officially in recession (e.g., United Kingdom, United States, Ireland, New Zealand, Germany, Japan). Job insecurities hit a high in 2008-2011 as fear regarding the future set in.

Then, with the pandemic, that job insecurity went through the roof. People were stood down, people lost their jobs, businesses closed (some permanently) and vaccine mandates meant that many were forced to resign if they did not wish to be injected.

Layoffs and retrenchments alone can create negative psychological and behavioural consequences – not only for the workers who are laid off, but for those who are left behind – not to mention the impact on close family and friends. Layoffs also usually increase workload for the remaining employees, while reducing their sense of job security.

I interviewed Jamie after he had completed some psychometrics as part of a recruitment process. He had had a number of careers, but his out-going, communicative personality really did suit him for sales where he also enjoyed the variety and activity related to that kind of role. He had worked as a trade specialist in sales selling tiles (indoor as well as outdoor) for over 5 years before moving to a trade company with a diversity of products such as roof sheeting, wall cladding, gutters, fencing and so forth.

However, he had noted a slow-down in the company due to poor management, where mistakes were being made, customer complaints were increasing and suppliers were beginning to put a stop on their accounts, goods and services. He then noted that a senior sales person who had been with the company for 17 years resigned and left to go elsewhere.

> Jamie said that he could see the company going under and
> that made him quite anxious so he decided to leave because
> he wanted to have "the choice of leaving" rather than wait
> for "things to fall over". (The company went into liquidation
> nine months later.)

2.4.4 Powerlessness and Less Control

The feeling of powerlessness is a universal cause of job
stress and is common to many of the most destructive stressors
in life.

The opposite of powerlessness in a job is autonomy which
motivates and drives us.[20] Powerlessness, on the other hand,
feeds the twin demons of depression: helplessness and
hopelessness.[21]

It comes as no surprise that workplace studies show that
occupations such as secretary, waitress, middle manager,
police officer, editor and medical intern are among the most
stressful occupations. What do these individuals have in
common? They're all required to respond to the demands and
timetables of others on a daily basis, with little control over their
own events. These individuals often complain that they have too
much responsibility, but too little authority.

Today's corporate economic upheavals, mergers and
restructuring often result in workers being moved to new
positions with sketchy job descriptions and unfamiliar or
ambiguous tasks. Workers often suddenly find themselves in
new work settings with new teams and new bosses.

Robert was the manager of finance in a federal government department that had a state head office. It was a good job in that he enjoyed the autonomy, the fact that he was on the senior management team, and that he reported directly to the state director.

However, certain changes in central office administration and hierarchy meant a restructuring of state office positions. Robert's job, for example, was amalgamated with human resources and the position re-titled "Manager, People Management". Because it was a 'new' position, he had to re-apply for his job.

Unfortunately, Robert was not successful in securing the position. What this meant, therefore, was that he was no longer on the senior management team, did not report directly to the state director, and instead, to add insult to injury, had to report to the successful applicant for the Manager, People Management position. He was also left with generally menial work which he did not find challenging or stimulating.

Robert felt that it was a "kick in the guts", and he felt demoralised and dejected. Not surprisingly, he was increasingly absent due to "sickness". He generally felt helpless in relation to his situation and could not see any light at the end of the tunnel. At times he became cynical and would say things like, "What's the use... no one around here cares anyway".

2.4.5 Lack of Good Leadership

Leaders make a difference – in all sorts of ways. Settings in which there is organisational confusion, or maybe an overly authoritarian, or even laissez-faire, or crisis-centred managerial style, are stressful. Excessive rules, red tape, and incompetent supervisors and co-workers can significantly increase stress.

One common failing of bad management is **a lack of feedback about performance**. Most employees really do want to do a good job. They need to be told when they're succeeding, and coached when they're not. As has been said before, *"Feedback is the breakfast of champions"*.

When managers don't invest time and effort in advising, coaching, training and listening, employee morale – and ultimately productivity – suffers.

What's also important to understand is that Generation Z (born 1995-2012 and who constitute about 34% of the workforce) and Generation Alpha (born 2013 and who constitute about 11% of the current workforce) both want leadership that is empowering and inspiring and which promotes their professional development. If companies can't or won't' recognise this, these generations will be out of there.

Of course, some managers and leaders will protest that they do not have enough time to undertake coaching or training of their staff. Sadly, they are unaware that if they did indeed put in the extra time and effort with their staff, there would be fewer crises, less turn-over, increased morale, and greater productivity.

What also makes productive employees is that they understand clearly what is expected of them on a daily basis. However, workplace surveys consistently reveal complaints from workers about **the lack of clarity about expectations**. Shifting management expectations create edgy, stressed, insecure employees who labour under the perception that they're failing. This pervasive sense of failure is one of the hallmarks of depression.

"People do not care what you know until they know that you care."

Author unknown

Employees also need to know that the boss cares about them as individuals, and most like to feel that they have an understanding boss they can turn to with problems.

Narelle had worked in a number of organisations, but in the last four years had worked as a School Services Officer (SSO) for the Department of Education in a secondary high school. She loved her job because she enjoyed helping people and with students in particular, she really felt that she was making a difference to young lives.

However, she saw me for assistance because she was becoming disillusioned with her workplace and the school leadership at various levels. For example, she still did not have a job description for her role (after 4 years). She felt that she was doing a good job, but she had never received feedback from her line manager at all and never had had a staff appraisal.

She said that the school leadership had also changed and that the principal was now "very business-like" and did not really connect at all with staff and didn't seem as though he really wanted to either. Overall, she said that "I feel like an after-thought at that school".

> She sought help for ways in which she could seek another job outside the education sector.

2.4.6 Lack of Social Support from Colleagues

We all need to have a sense of belonging. It's a basic need. You can't get away from it.

Employees need to feel involved in the workplace community and invested in the organisation's success. Being isolated and ostracised can lead to negativistic thinking and ultimately depression. The lockdowns due to the covid-19 pandemic highlighted the impact of separation.

The Gallup Organisation now has a database that includes 10 million employee and manager interviews conducted in 41 languages across 114 countries. This database was analysed to find which aspects of work were the most powerful in explaining workers' motivations on the job.

Of the twelve elements of work life that emerged as the core of the unwritten social contract between employee and employer, ninth on the list was, "My associates or fellow employees are committed to doing quality work". Tenth on the list was, "I have a best friend at work". Both have to do with the importance of a collegiate spirit and interaction among peers.[22]

When people are not permitted to participate in problem-solving or contribute to management or team discussions, they don't feel valued or valuable. No one wants to feel that they are an expendable commodity or that they don't count. "*They wouldn't miss me if I were gone",* is a refrain frequently heard from depressed workers.

2.4.7 Hazardous Work Environment

Poor or uncomfortable work settings can create both physical and emotional stress. Factors include hazardous chemicals, noise, lack of privacy, poor lighting, cramped conditions, poor ventilation, poor temperature control, and inadequate sanitary facilities. They all count.

2.4.8 Workplace Bullying

Bullying is a significant contributor to workplace depression and anxiety. From 2007 to 2021, Zogby International have conducted thousands of interviews in conjunction with the Workplace Bullying Institute (WBI).[23] The latest WBI-Zogby survey revealed:

- 30% of workers have been bullied (compared to 19% in 2017)
- 43% of remote workers have been bullied (50% in meetings and 9% via email)
- 21% of bullies are co-workers
- 65% of bullies are bosses
- 67% of the bullies are male and 33% are female

It's estimated that 40% of bullied employees suffer in silence, never telling their employers. Only 3% of them go so far as to file a lawsuit. Tolerance of bullying is ultimately expensive to employers when you take into account turnover costs, absenteeism, lost productivity and health care claims.

Workplace bullying typically falls into one of five categories.[24] What are those categories?

1. **Threat to professional status**

   e.g., belittling, criticising or devaluing someone's skills

2. **Threat to personal standing**

   e.g., mocking a handicap, personal mannerism or aspect of the person's private life, or making a derogatory reference to age or physical characteristics -- this is usually the most psychologically damaging form of bullying

3. **Isolation**

   e.g., preventing participation, withholding information, or keeping someone out of the loop

4. **Overwork**

   e.g., imposing an impossible deadline or forcing someone to work long hours

5. **Destabilization**

   e.g., removing responsibility or shifting a worker's responsibilities in a way that sets them up to fail

When victims do report bullying, some managers are tempted to write it off glibly as a "personality clash". Using this kind of label is either ignorance or just a cheap shot at trying to off-load the problem. Marginalising the experience has the effect of blaming the victim rather than the bully or the workplace environment that tolerates bullying. Bullied victims can eventually fall into the clutches of learned helplessness.

Research in Sweden has shown that a significant proportion of people who commit suicide have a history of being bullied at work.[25]

Maria was a 51-year-old teacher who taught both French and Italian to various classes in elementary and primary school. She seemed relatively pleasant and friendly, at least in the context of the psychologist's office, although there was a hint that she was somewhat timid and hesitant at times.

She recited that there had been pressure on space in her school, together with a general cutback in resources, especially in regards to the teaching of foreign languages. While on yard duty, she was approached by the deputy principal and informed that her resource room would be shifted to a deserted end of the school and that due to funding issues, her programs may well be cut back. This seemed to be the final straw that broke the camel's back.

Maria responded in writing the next day to the leadership team of the school, indicating that she felt she had not been given appropriate time to consider the move nor had she had any input into the decision, and she felt this was just a continuation of situations in which she felt targeted.

She informed me, for example, that in staff meetings she had felt singled out, that the leadership team had been maneuvering for some time to restrict her programs, that plans for the school curriculum (including foreign languages) had been drawn up without her input, that she had been left off certain committees relevant to her area, and that she had been asked to take on relief classes more than was considered appropriate.

In essence, she felt that she had been bullied, especially by the leadership group, including the principal and her deputy.

> She said she had had enough. She had experienced sleep disturbance for some months, had often slept most of the weekend, found it extremely difficult to get up in the mornings and go to school, had dropped in weight, and had also been quite teary at home with her family.
>
> Maria became very tearful in my office and felt that there was no way out. She thought that perhaps the only avenue was to take sick leave or perhaps go on WorkCover. She was at a loss.

2.4.9 Death of a Co-worker

Co-workers can become an extended family of sorts. At the least, they become very friendly and feel connected to each other. The death of a co-worker, therefore, may be grieved deeply by employees, particularly if the death was sudden and tragic, or occurred in the workplace. In production and manufacturing environments, preoccupation with a co-worker's death can become a safety hazard for workers operating equipment, performing delicate operations, or monitoring product quality.

2.4.10 Traumatic Events on the Job

Some occupations are inherently dangerous – police officers, firefighters, ambulance drivers, military personnel, and disaster specialists, to name a few. These individuals witness terrible, tragic events and may be exposed to personal danger on a daily basis. This perpetual heavy stress load can lead to sleep disturbance, guilt, fearfulness, negative ruminations, and a myriad of physical complaints.

Even ordinary jobs can suddenly become traumatic, for instance when a co-worker, boss, customer or member of the public physically threatens an employee, an employee is robbed or taken hostage, a workplace shooting occurs or there is a hazardous materials accident or perhaps a fire occurs.

Such events can trigger initial panic and terror followed by widespread depression among employees and even post-traumatic stress disorder (PTSD).

2.4.11 Lack of Down Time

Many of us work while at home or on vacation. Even when we're not working, we're working. There is no "down" time.

We answer emails, phone calls and faxes. In fact, 81% of email users admit to checking their email daily while on vacation.[26] While technology has dramatically improved our lives, the ceaseless use of technology can boost our stress levels.

As Martin Moore-Ede writes in his 1993 book, *The Twenty-Four-Hour Society*:

"Our bodies were designed to hunt by day, sleep at night and never travel more than a few dozen miles from sunrise to sunset. Now we work and play at all hours, whisk off by jet to the far side of the globe, make life-or-death decisions or place orders on foreign stock exchanges in the wee hours of the morning. The pace of technological innovation is outstripping the ability of the human race to understand the consequences.

> We are machine-centred in our thinking – focused on the
> optimisation of technology and equipment – rather than human-
> centered – focused on the optimisation of human alertness and
> performance."

In other words, technology has dictated how we live life. Instead of having periods of peak performance followed by rest periods, we seem to be constantly on an "up", and not coming down to relax or chill out. The consequences are dire, and a bit like running a car flat-out with no service, maintenance check or re-tune.

2.5 Reason 3: More People Being Treated

One contributing factor to the workplace depression statistics may simply be that more people are emerging from the shadows to seek treatment for depression. In fact, two-thirds of U.S. workers say they are likely to seek help for stress.

2.5.1 Psychoeducation

Depression has become a mainstream topic, thanks to concerted efforts to promote public awareness by government agencies, private foundations, the media, and even celebrities who have been willing to openly discuss their battles with depression. People have a better awareness of symptoms and treatments. In fact, 35% of Americans give the media the most credit for reducing the stigma surrounding mental health services.[3]

The internet is also a vast information resource. People can educate themselves about depression in the privacy of their own homes, which helps demystify the illness, make it seem less scary, and foster a sense of hope for recovery.

2.5.2 Destigmatisation

The stigma attached to psychological disorders has historically deterred the public from seeking – and companies from wanting to pay for – treatment or therapy. Stigma has not only deprived people of treatment, it has deprived them of dignity and interfered with their full participation in society.[27]

The destigmatisation of depression increases the number of treated cases. Almost 50% of Americans believe the stigma of seeking mental health services has decreased. About 91% say they would consult or recommend that a family member consult a mental health professional.[3]

Late 19th and early 20th century medicine separated the mental health treatment system from mainstream health care. More and more, depression has become widely viewed as a combination of both physical and psychological dysfunction, which has helped lessen the stigma of depressive disorders.

Frank walked into my office and sat down. He was a well-built 35-year-old whose body frame clearly evidenced the fact that he was strong, with a good physique. He reported that he had been a plumber, and had worked hard until he hurt his back. This, he said, was a major blow in that not only did he have to give up his career, as well as his part-time job as a security guard, but he also had to give up all the things that he loved, such as football, weight training, and extreme sports such as rock climbing. He said that his whole identity as a man had been taken from him.

He went on to say that he felt like he had "lost himself", and that he had become grumpy with his partner at home and was not a nice person to live with. His general practitioner had previously suggested that he might be depressed, but Frank waved his hand through the air as he talked to me and said that he didn't "believe any of that stuff, and only wimps get depressed…besides, what would all my mates think?"

On the previous weekend, however, his partner had announced that she was moving out and that she could not take any more of his tantrums, ugly moods and general grumpiness. Frank was devastated. He loved this woman and she was gone, at least for now. He was clearly in pain – emotional pain.

As he sat across from me and looked down at his hands, he simply said, "Maybe the doc was right, maybe I am depressed". He continued, saying, "I didn't think guys got depressed…I thought it was just a woman's thing."

2.5.3 Expanded Insurance Coverage

Treatment has become more affordable for workers whose health insurance covers treatment for depression, a policy that has, in many countries, been mandated by government legislation.

In 1997, for example, the United States Congress added depression to the Americans with Disabilities Act (ADA) as a covered medical condition. However, it's worth noting that in the U.S., 87% of Americans still cite lack of insurance coverage as a top reason for not seeking mental health services.[3]

In Australia however, Medicare which is the federal government's insurance health care scheme, added psychologist visits in 2016 as being covered. Psychiatrist's visits had traditionally been covered by Medicare, while the introduction of psychologists allowed for people to have 10 visits in any one year.

2.5.4 Employee Assistance Programs

Many organisations have employee assistance programs, which offer free confidential diagnostics and counselling or treatment by independent providers who are trained professional counsellors, psychologists or social workers.

With concern about rising health care costs and lost productivity resulting from depressive disorders (among other things), employers are increasingly willing to invest in educating their workforces about mental health issues and in offering direct assistance.

Today in the U.S., 40-60% of worksites with more than fifty employees offer some type of mental health program.[28] Figures are similar or better for other westernised countries. For example, in Australia, EAPs are available to about 80% of Australia's top 500 companies as well as small to medium organisations, but lower for private sector organisations.[29]

Over the last ten years, there has been an increasing acknowledgment of the role of the workplace in promoting or hindering mental wellness, and many employers are actively promoting good mental health in the workplace.

2.6 Reason 4: More Effective Treatments

Governments worldwide have devoted more money to research about what is effective in relation to health and well-being (including mental health issues).

Scientific advancements and new technology have given us medications that are more effective and have fewer side effects. Clinicians in the mental health care sector have developed, refined and documented better therapeutic techniques.

The net result is that more people are being treated more effectively, which gives hope and assurance to others in the community who may have been suffering in silence.

2.7 Reason 5: More Protection for Individuals with Mental Illness

Today's workers feel more comfortable about seeking treatment without fear of losing their jobs. Recent legislation has acknowledged that the workforce includes many individuals with psychiatric disabilities who may have previously faced employment discrimination because their disabilities were stigmatised or misunderstood, and has also moved toward providing more legal protection for those suffering from depressive disorders.

Countries like the U.K., U.S. and Australia have laws which emphasise the individual's rights and anti-discrimination. For example, Title 1 of the U.S. Americans with Disabilities Act (ADA), and the British Disability Discrimination Act (DDA) of 1995, combat employment discrimination on the basis of psychiatric disability, as well as the myths, fears, and stereotypes upon which discrimination is based.

In Australia, it is the Disability Discrimination and Other Human Rights Legislation Amendment Bill 2008, which updates the Disability Discrimination Act (DDA) of 1992 regarding unlawful discrimination against people with disabilities.

The increased visibility of the disability rights movement and the impact of anti-discrimination legislation have encouraged today's employers to take a proactive approach to battling depression in the workplace. (For more information on legal compliance, see Chapter 7.)

Chapter 2 Summary

Certainly, workplace depression has always existed. But for many employers, escalating disability claims and diminished productivity leave no doubt that the incidence of depression in the workplace is increasing. Medical research backs this up.

Depression is no respecter of professions in that a survey in Australia noted that there were higher than average depression scores among professionals, especially lawyers, as well as a significant use of alcohol and other non-prescription drugs to manage the feelings of overwhelm, sadness and depression.

There is no single explanation for depression's escalation in the workplace. But we know some of the reasons, and addressing those is a good place to start.

Reason 1: Overall stress levels in life have increased

The stress of modern life is increasing at an alarming rate: 45% over the last thirty years, according to some surveys.

Reason 2: Workplace stress has increased due to:

- Insufficient wages
- High daily mental load and high productivity demands
- Job insecurity
- Powerlessness and less control over job responsibilities
- Lack of good leadership
- Lack of social support from colleagues
- Uncomfortable or hazardous work environments
- Workplace bullying
- Death of a co-worker
- Traumatic events on the job
- Even when we're not working, we're working

Reason 3: More people are being treated

One contributing factor to workplace depression statistics may simply be that more people are emerging from the shadows to seek treatment for depression. In fact, two-thirds of U.S. workers say they are likely to seek help for stress. Further contributions to increased treatment include:

- Psychoeducation
- Destigmatisation
- Accessibility and affordability through insurance coverage
- Employee assistance programs

Reason 4: More effective treatments

Governments worldwide have devoted more money to research. Scientific advancements and new technology have given us medications that are more effective and have fewer side effects.

Clinicians in the mental health care sector have developed, refined and documented better therapeutic techniques. The net result is that more people are being treated more effectively, which gives hope and assurance to others in the community who may have been suffering in silence.

Reason 5: More Protection for Individuals with Mental Illness

Recent legislation has acknowledged that the workforce includes many individuals with psychiatric disabilities who may have previously faced employment discrimination.

"The term clinical depression finds its way into too many conversations these days. One has a sense that a catastrophe has occurred in the psychic landscape."

Leonard Cohen, 1934-
Canadian singer-songwriter, musician, poet,
novelist and artist

CHAPTER 3

What Is Depression?

Introduction

These days, everyone believes they know what depression is – what it looks like, how it behaves. Depression, after all, has become a frequent topic of discussion, a phenomenon fuelled, in part, by talk shows, podcasts, social and mainstream media. But the truth is that depression can take many forms.[1] The symptoms, severity and course that depression follows varies widely from individual to individual.

The word "depression" is loosely used. People may say that they are depressed when they are simply upset, angry, frustrated, or just experiencing a normal period of feeling down.

A friend of mine went to visit his long-time friend who had been hospitalised with severe clinical depression. Needless to say, it was a confronting visit in many ways. Riding home on the train he overheard the guys behind him talking.

One said, "Oh, I'm so depressed. The fridge broke down this morning and now I need to either get a repairman out or buy a new one."

He felt like turning around and saying to him, "Look buddy, if you think that you're depressed, you ought to see where I've just come from."

In relation to knowledge and attitudes, a survey in Australia in 2007 asked about people's perception of depression.[2] Anecdotally, not much has changed since then. What is interesting is that there was a lack of understanding about the complex nature of depression, with over half the sample surveyed (58%) indicating that *"People with depression should simply identify the cause of depression and remove the cause."* It's simply not that easy. What this says though, is that the general population has a simplistic view of depression which, importantly, may well impact the way that depressives are managed in the work setting.

"Depression is rage spread thin."

George Santayana, 1863-1952
Spanish citizen, philosopher, poet and novelist

3.1 Normal Mood Swings or Normal Depression

Most of us feel out of sorts at times. We may feel sad or miserable. This is fairly normal, and generally follows a disappointment, a financial down-turn, a job loss, the loss of a friend, or any number of other life events which can be stressful.

These kinds of feelings are natural and are experienced by everyone at some point in their lives. We call this "**normal depression**", or a "normal depressive mood state".

This normal depression can be experienced as a "blue" mood, a lack of interest or pleasure in things, being "down" on yourself and self-critical, a lack of self-confidence, wanting to give up, or having a gloomy outlook for the future. These feelings are not generally intensive or held at great depth, are not disabling, and are not permanent, lasting only a few hours to a few days or perhaps a week or so.

Most of us recover relatively quickly from these set-backs, especially if we have other good things happening in our lives, we have a supportive network, or if we are generally a positive or resilient sort of person.

Sometimes it's difficult to determine when an individual has crossed that line that separates normal mood fluctuations from a serious mood pathology. As you become more attuned to spotting the symptoms of depression (see the lists below in this chapter), you'll discover that many people exhibit some depressive symptoms, yet **they do not meet the criteria for a diagnosis** of clinical depression.

A person may, for example, periodically exhibit two or three of the criteria required for a severe depressive episode for a week or so. You might notice that a particular employee has lost weight, seems tired lately, is perhaps even complaining of insomnia, and feeling "out of sorts" or "blue".

What should you do? Simply continue to observe. Look for behavioural patterns that repeat. Look for additional symptoms, and symptoms that continue for more than two weeks. Be careful not to overreact.

Your approach to managing individuals who are subclinical for depression may include some of the same initial strategies you would use for individuals who are ultimately diagnosed with clinical depression. We will get into these strategies especially in Chapters 7 and 9.

3.2 Clinical Depression

Some people continue to feel miserable and down for long periods of time, even when there is no obvious reason for feeling that way. This is called "**clinical depression**", in which the "down" mood state and the associated symptoms (see the Nine Main Symptoms of Depression on the next few pages as well as Table 3.1) are present for **more than two weeks**, and are accompanied by social and psychological problems.

Often friends and family realise that the person is feeling low and try to jolly them out if it, but to no avail. Even when something good happens, the person doesn't acknowledge it and it does little to cheer them up.

Although there is often an event or situation that triggers clinical depression, sometimes people become depressed for reasons that cannot always be determined. In the beginning, these people just feel unmotivated, sluggish, or even just tired. But as their depression worsens, they become less and less motivated, to the point where they struggle to get out of bed and get dressed in the morning.

So what is depression then? Depression is characterised by a mood disturbance. In other words, it is typically experienced as **a significantly poorer than normal mood for an extended period of time (i.e., beyond two weeks)**. It's important to understand that depression is not just feeling a bit flat over a few hours, or even for a day or two. That's considered normal.

Instead, this down mood is a prolonged emotion that doesn't go away. It's when these feelings linger, consuming our thoughts day in and day out, that the condition becomes clinically significant.

It can last weeks, months, and sometimes years. It is a pervasive emotion that infiltrates every part of our lives and colours our view of the world. Depression is like wearing a pair of sunglasses that taints our whole view of the world.

Is depression a mental illness? The short answer is yes.

Episodes of depression often follow a severe stressor in life, such as the death of a loved one, marital separation, a divorce, or bankruptcy. Research shows that these kinds of events can often play a significant role in the precipitation of the first, or perhaps second episode of depression, and tend to play less of a role in subsequent episodes.

An untreated depressive episode typically lasts four months or longer, regardless of age of the person. In 70-80% of cases, there is a complete remission of symptoms and functioning returns to normal.

In 20-30% of cases though, some depressive symptoms remain, although they no longer meet the criteria for a major depressive episode. These symptoms may persist for months or years.

Note, too, that clinical depression has a high rate of recurrence:

- At least 60% of people who experience a single major depressive episode can be expected to experience a second episode.
- People who have had two episodes have a 70% chance of having a third.
- People who have had three episodes have a 90% chance of having a fourth episode.[1]

"Depression is inertia."

Dr Wayne Dyer, 1940-
American psychologist, author and speaker

3.3 The Nine Main Symptoms of Depression

1. Feeling miserable

This feeling of being sad, hopeless, discouraged or empty goes on **for a period of at least two weeks**. This can be a single depressive episode, or episodes can recur over time.

Even a laundry list of symptoms cannot paint a realistic portrait of true depression. At its worst, depression is a bleak, black existence that feels, to the sufferer, inevitable, insurmountable and eternal. Depression is a lonely place, devoid of hope and joy. Depressives ultimately stop expecting positive outcomes. Even when something good happens, they are often unable to recognise it, and too numb to enjoy or appreciate it.

One of the least understood aspects of depression is that the deepest, darkest depression is not experienced as melancholy or sadness. The most severe depression – and most alarming – is **numbness**, a complete absence of feeling and complete loss of concern for oneself.

To the severely depressed employee, receiving a substantial, long-anticipated promotion may not feel much different from getting a good parking place. Conversely, losing that promotion may not feel much worse than burning the toast at breakfast.

In many cases, mood is significantly worse in the morning, then improves somewhat as the day wears on, a condition known as *diurnal variation*.

Sometimes anxiety leads to depression, and sometimes depression is evidenced by increased irritability or anger (e.g., having a short fuse, anger outbursts, blaming others, or heightened frustration or eruption over seemingly minor events).

2. **Loss of interest and enjoyment**
   Depressives lose the sense of pleasure from activities they used to enjoy. Loss of interest or pleasure is nearly universal among depressed individuals. They are no longer interested in hobbies, sports, favourite pastimes, and even sexual relations.

   Occasionally, there is also a fearfulness of people, activities or objects, often leading to a withdrawal from a variety of activities, friends and family.

3. **Loss of appetite and weight**

There is usually a loss of weight – usually 2-3 kgs (4-7 lbs.) – due to a loss of appetite. Occasionally it's the other way around, and the depressive eats more and puts on weight.

4. **Sleep difficulties**

There is either restlessness, inability to get to sleep, or early morning awakening, even though one might be feeling exhausted or be sleeping more than usual.

Often depressives awaken early in the morning, long before it's time to arise. However, some may actually sleep more than usual. More than three-fourths of depressives report trouble with sleep. According to the *DSM-V-TR*, sleep EEG abnormalities are evident in 40-60% of outpatients, and in up to 90% of inpatients with a major depressive episode.[1]

5. **Changed movements and speech**

You may notice a marked pause before someone with depression answers a question or initiates an action that has been requested. This is called *psychomotor retardation*. Speech may be very quiet, even inaudible. Some depressives even stop speaking completely, except to respond to a direct question. To this end, the person could well become totally mute.

Furthermore, movements may be slowed, and they may have a stooped posture or perhaps be staring into space.

At the other extreme are depressed individuals who are so anxious that they become agitated, which may be expressed as hand-wringing, pacing, or an inability to sit still.

6. Loss of energy

Even when they are not physically active, depressed people usually complain of fatigue, which they may report as tiredness or loss of energy. Even the smallest tasks require substantial effort. For example, just getting up and getting dressed in the morning can be exhausting, and take twice as long as usual.

7. Recurring unpleasant thoughts

Depressives experience thoughts about guilt, being a bad or worthless person, and about wanting to die. They lose the ability to objectively evaluate themselves, a symptom which often manifests as low self-esteem, or feelings of worthlessness or guilt. Guilt may include unrealistically negative evaluations of one's worth, or guilty preoccupations with and ruminations over minor past failings. There is a tendency to completely misinterpret events to the point that one believes a particular event is evidence of one's personal defects, or that one is somehow responsible for the event.

A real estate agent, for example, may blame himself, and beat up on himself for the drop in his sales, when it is the market itself that has dropped significantly, and other agents are also not able to make sales. Another person may believe that somehow or other they are responsible for world poverty. They may slip into a persistent negative feedback loop, constantly pointing to their personal misfortunes. They always see the down-side. They are negative. They may misinterpret neutral or trivial day-to-day events as evidence of personal defects.

They may assume an exaggerated or even inappropriate sense of responsibility for negative events. For example, an accountant may blame herself for failing to meet budget, when there has been an overall rise in company overheads due to world fuel price increases (or similar). The sense of worthlessness or guilt may even be of delusional proportions.

8. Inability to concentrate
Along with slow, inefficient or even cloudy thinking, the inability to concentrate makes decision-making and planning difficult.

Many depressed individuals become cognitively impaired, unable to think, organise, remember information or make decisions, even simple decisions. They may be easily distracted and unable to concentrate on the task at hand.

A computer programmer, for example, may no longer be able to perform complicated, but previously manageable tasks.

9. Thoughts of death or suicide
These thoughts are sometimes accompanied by a specific plan of how to die and sometimes not. These

thoughts come about from the belief that others would be better off if the person were dead. The tendency is to give up in the face of perceived insurmountable obstacles, or to want to end what is seen as an extremely painful emotional state which appears to be never-ending.

Traditionally speaking, **severe** clinical depression is characterised by **at least five of these symptoms being evident over at least a two week period**.

The symptoms have to cause significant distress in the person's social life or work life, or in any other important aspect of living.

Milder clinical depression is characterised by **two to four of these symptoms**.

To repeat, the symptoms must be present nearly every day for at least two weeks.

Remember too that most of us can feel down for hours or a few days due to particular circumstances or events, but we tend to bounce back after that time. This is what is considered quite normal.

It is when the "blues" continue for over two weeks and five of these categories listed above can be identified that we then move out of "normalcy".

"Depression is an absolute monster. It can take over your life and you can completely lose sight of the person you were before you became ill.

Without doubt, it is the worst thing that has ever happened to me. I lost four years of my life to this foul illness and it is very scary and threatening for me to look back on those terrible times.

I will always be in debt to my caring and kind doctor for identifying my problem and then helping me battle through periods of hell to where I am now.

I did not respond immediately to treatment. That was scary too. I had to really work on the management of my illness – but it was worth it.

I really would like to say that people should never give up hope or lose hope. I probably would've if it hadn't been for my GP and those around me.

I'm not sure at this stage, but maybe I will be managing my illness for the rest of my life, but who cares? At least I have a life to live.

The fact that I may be on a low dose of medication for life is a small cost to pay for the joy of not thinking about killing myself on a daily basis."

Table 3.1

Diagnosis: More than two weeks of persistent depressed mood and/or loss of interest or pleasure PLUS symptoms in at least 3 of the following categories:

PHYSICAL	BEHAVIORAL	THOUGHTS	FEELINGS
Tiredness	Withdrawal	Negative thinking	Overwhelmed
Appetite / weight change	Unproductive	"Hopeless, helpless & worthless"	Unhappy
Headaches	Alcohol / Sedatives	Suicidal thoughts	Guilty
Disturbed sleep	Stop enjoyable activities		Indecisive
Sick / run down	Concentration difficulties		Disappointed
Movements slowed or agitated	Impulsiveness & recklessness		No confidence
			Irritable

Beyond Blue website in Australia indicates that this table could be used as a quick guide to diagnosing depression.

It also needs to be understood that while the nine symptoms listed above, together with the symptoms listed in Table 3.1, may indicate depression, most by themselves do not. For example, disturbed sleep could be due to a number of factors such as general stress in one's life, a snoring partner or a weak bladder.

Ultimately too, there is perhaps no such thing as a "mind-body split." Our mental states and physical states are inextricably bound. We are all connected! The psychological or cognitive symptoms of depression – *what we think about* – are just as important as the physiological ones, and any diagnosis and treatment plan must consider both.

The Dark Clouds at Work is not intended to be a diagnostic tool. However, in order to help you understand how to treat, manage and coexist with depression in the workplace, we need to first pinpoint what depression is...and isn't. Even in this age of "depression enlightenment", clinical depression can be misdiagnosed, and certainly, unfortunately, undiagnosed.

For psychologists, psychiatrists and social workers treating depressives, it is critical to formally assess symptoms and draw careful clinical distinctions. What these professionals typically use is a text such as the *Diagnostic and Statistical Manual of Mental Disorders,* known as the *DSM,* which is an international classificatory system published by the American Psychiatric Association for determining psychiatric, psychological and mental health disorders. It is periodically updated with current statistics and the latest research findings.

The current version is the *DSM-V-TR* and its coding system, which is used in clinical records and insurance forms, is used in the U.S. as well as in other parts of the world such as Australia. The other major resource that is used is the *International Statistical Classification of Diseases and Related Health Problems (ICD-11),* which is published by the World Health Organisation. The *ICD* is used typically throughout the European countries.

(If you wish to view the clinical criteria that warrant a diagnosis of major depressive episode according to the *DSM-V-TR*, please see Appendix A. The person must meet at least five of the nine symptoms.)

For organisations that need to manage depressives in the workplace environment, it's important to simply be able to recognise **the red flags of depression** in order to stop a treatable problem from escalating to a disastrous and possibly irreparable dynamic.

3.4 The Features of Depression at Work

What could you expect to see in the workplace? Certainly not the full list of nine symptoms that have been described above, because not all of them would be observable.

For managers and HR professionals, it's important to be aware that, of the various consequences of depression, the impact on occupational functioning may be the hardest to detect. Why? Because **earning a livelihood is so important that most people will go to great lengths to hide symptoms** that could threaten their employment. Obviously, this makes the job of early detection harder.

Understanding the criteria used by clinicians to diagnose a major depressive episode will help you learn to **spot the red flags of depression**. Stay alert for the following at work:

1. **A sad, miserable or dejected employee**
   You will notice a change in their demeanour, not overnight of course, but over weeks or months you will notice that they are not as they used to be. They are less out-going, less cheerful, and they may look downcast.

Watch out, too, for those who increasingly show temper outbursts or anger, and who increasingly get frustrated and annoyed, often over little things. This is the flip-side of depression; bursts of anger followed by a period of being flat and depressed.

2. **Tiredness, fatigue and low energy**
    They will carry their body differently and show signs of lethargy. Perhaps they may arrive at work late on a more frequent basis or take off more sick days than usual.

3. **General appearance**
    People often drop weight (or occasionally put it on), and their clothes, hair or make-up may become less neat and tidy.

4. **Sleep difficulties**
    They may mention that they are having trouble sleeping, or they may be late to work increasingly because they "slept in" or "the alarm didn't go off". They may also look tired, drawn around the eyes, and yawn a good deal.

5. **Inability to concentrate or thinking difficulties**
    These symptoms will be evident as people start to forget details that they previously would not have, or they miss deadlines that were relatively obvious, or their performance drops off significantly.

6. **Withdrawal from the team or workplace**
    They may stop socialising at the water cooler or the coffee machine, not go into the staff room for morning coffee break or lunch or make excuses not to attend the Friday night drinks get-together.

3.5 Distinguishing Depressive Conditions

Certainly, we can have a diagnosis of clinical depression, and traditionally professionals have indicated that such can be measured on a scale from "mild" through "moderate" to "severe", but can we categorize depression any further than that? Professor Gordon Parker and his research team at the Black Dog Institute say we can.[3] He provides a unique model of clinical depression and argues that **determining the "sub-types" of depression is critical to both diagnosis and treatment**.

As we know, clinical depression is more severe than a normal depressed state or normal mood swings, since it lasts for more than two weeks and affects functioning at home and/or work. However, Professor Gordon Parker suggests that there are **three** categories of clinical depression as follows:

- **Non-melancholic depression**
  Characterised by depressed mood lasting more than two weeks which affects functioning at home and/or work. However, there is **no psychomotor disturbance** (e.g., slowed movements or speech, or agitated movements) and **no psychotic features** (e.g., hallucinations).

- **Melancholic depression**
  Characterised by severely depressed mood **plus psychomotor disturbance**, but **no psychotic features**.

- **Psychotic melancholia**
  Characterised by severe depressed mood **plus psychomotor disturbance as well as psychotic features** (e.g., delusions and hallucinations).

Let's look at each category now in more detail.

3.5.1 Non-melancholic Depression

Up to 90% of people diagnosed with clinical depression fall into this category.

This kind of depression affects about one in four women and one in six men in the Western world over their lifetime.

This type of depression is brought about by a combination of personality characteristics or temperament coupled with life stressors (e.g., the death of a loved one, retrenchment, marital separation, divorce, or financial difficulties). Sometimes added to the mix are poor coping styles and negative thinking habits. These people report being depressed, usually with low self-esteem, and are self-critical and experience many of the nine symptoms listed above, such as sleep disturbance and change in appetite.

Genetic factors and biological factors may also play a role in the development of this form of depression, but their contribution is thought to be minimal. Non-melancholic depression may, at times, be a more serious form of normal sadness. However, the duration and persistence of symptoms beyond two weeks and the disruptive influence on work, home and social functioning highlights the need for immediate intervention and help.

In contrast with the other two depressive categories, people with **non-melancholic depression do not show any evidence of psychomotor disturbance or psychotic symptoms**. Not surprisingly, people with non-melancholic depression can often be cheered up to some degree and are less likely to report significant concentration or memory problems.

Interestingly, Parker and his associates have determined that those with certain personality characteristics are more prone to non-melancholic depression when **triggered by life stressors**.[3] However, the following particular temperaments or **personality styles** only serve to exacerbate any triggers that might occur:

- **Anxious worrier**; gets stressed easily, worries about minor issues, stews over anticipated problems, has self-doubts, is pessimistic regarding the future

- **Irritable person**; gets rattled easily, is impatient with others, gets irritable or explodes when stressed, lashes out, criticises others, indulges in reckless behaviour such as drinking or gambling

- **Self-focused personality**; is non-empathic, has a lack of consideration for others, has a tendency to blame others, sometimes is narcissistic or anti-social, has anger or hostility towards others

- **Perfectionistic personality**; obsesses, is very self-disciplined, plans ahead, attempts to control the environment to reduce stress levels, pushes to be the best, ruminates over past behaviours and future actions, procrastinates or avoids making decisions

- **Social avoidance personality**; is shy and self-conscious, hangs back, withdraws from others when stressed

- **Personal reserve personality**; avoids self-disclosure or honest reflection, tends to be formal, polite and reserved in dealing with others, withdraws from social interactions when distressed

- **Sensitive personality**; is highly sensitive to rejection, is acutely aware of what others say and do, especially about them, bases their self-esteem on what others think of them, feels empty, engages in self-consoling behaviours

- **Self-critical personality**; is never good enough, feels it's always their fault, has low self-esteem, struggles to find any successes in their life, harbours feelings of worthlessness, relies on others to make decisions when stressed

In terms of treatment for the non-melancholic person, response rates to treatment approaches are all very similar even though the treatments might be quite different (e.g., anti-depressant drugs, psychotherapy and counselling).

Sandra was a 33-year-old clerk in the public service. She first saw a psychologist when she was 12 years old because her mother felt that she was not socialising properly or fitting in with the other children at school. She had had a number of depressive episodes since that time.

More recently, Sandra had had "a falling out" with a work colleague, and since then had become very withdrawn and pre-occupied. She had also become anxious and reticent about leaving the house. She reported that, generally speaking, she usually avoided social situations because she felt embarrassed and uncomfortable around people. She described herself as "a bit shy".

Her family felt that there was something wrong, but Sandra would not tell them what it might be. Sandra was also isolating herself in her room and not interacting with the family, tended to stay in bed, and if anyone called, she told the family to say that she was out and not at home.

Sandra had previously been reliable and steady as a person, but she was now stewing on her issues, her responsibilities were being neglected, and she also felt very guilty for letting her family down.

3.5.2 Melancholic Depression

Melancholic depression occurs in about 5-10% of the population.

The mood state is more severe than that of non-melancholic depression. The depressed mood lasts for more than two weeks and involves moderate to severe social impairment, together with **psychomotor disturbance** (e.g., stooped in posture, slow movements, staring into space). The psychomotor disturbance can also be associated with an agitated state, such as not being able to sit still. There is a loss of pleasure and a general empty feeling, and often the mood and energy level are worse in the morning; the person has difficulty getting up, but symptoms improve later in the day.

The origins of this kind of depression are primarily **biological and genetic**, and the depressive may have a significant family history of depression. Spontaneous remission is highly unlikely. While the first few episodes may develop as a result of stress factors in the person's life, later episodes could well occur "out of the blue".

In terms of treatment for the melancholic depressive, the response rate to physical treatments such as anti-depressant drugs is high, but is generally minimal to counselling or psychotherapy.

"I really felt lost without my wife. It's the old saying, that you never really appreciate someone or something until you lose them or haven't got it any more.

I think I was depressed for about three years or so after she died. I tried to struggle on, but I knew in the end that I wasn't coping.

I had no energy, felt that all my limbs were slowing up and I got to a point where I hardly spoke. I remember feeling this way too for a good period of time when my father died.

A friend of mine took me out for a few meals and then finally suggested that I ought to see my GP to see if he'd recommend anything.

It's so hard to explain what this 'black cloud' is all about, but it really stuffs your life up. It takes over your whole being. It was like a heavy load where I couldn't think straight or think properly and I couldn't feel much either.

I used to feel quite embarrassed about the chemist knowing that I was depressed, being a professional in the way that I was with such standing in the community. It seemed like every time, too, that I went into that pharmacy, I got served by this young female

> 'bitch' who would just give me what seemed like a judgmental
> look when handing over the prescription. I don't know if she
> thought I was faking depression or what, but hellfire, she sure
> made it tough for me."

3.5.3 Psychotic Melancholia

This is an extremely severe form of depression and is
thought to originate from disruptions in neural circuits and brain
neurochemistry. It occurs in about 1-2% of the population, and
can often appear later in life.

As well as the depressed mood and psychomotor
disturbance evident in melancholic depression, psychotic
melancholic depression has **the added features of delusions
and hallucinations** ("My thoughts are being controlled from
outer space", "Others can hear what I'm thinking"), or over-
valued ideas ("I'm responsible for the economic crisis in my
country"), most involving pathological expressions of guilt.

Treatment involves physical and biological approaches, with
the older anti-depressants being more effective than the newer
ones. However, anti-depressants alone are not as effective as
a combination of anti-psychotic medication and electroconvulsive therapy in some cases.

> Police were called to a junior elementary school where one
> of the teachers had locked a student in a cupboard. Jane
> was a 29-year-old Grade 2 teacher who had recently
> returned from six weeks of maternity leave. She had been
> teaching at her elementary school since she graduated at

the age of 23 years. She was well-respected and liked by students and parents alike. Her performance appraisals had always been positive and she'd gotten on well with other staff.

However, since returning to work she had been "different". Her students had been commenting that she was ignoring them and "being weird", and the school assistant had observed that Jane was frequently late to school and often lost her concentration in class. The principal had noted that Jane was behind in her paperwork and had missed several deadlines.

One of her teacher friends noted that Jane had become very suspicious of both the students and her colleagues and that she had found Jane in the staff bathroom crying.

When the police arrived at the school, they found Jane in the classroom with her head down, sitting in front of the cupboard with the child locked inside. The officers knelt down beside her and introduced themselves and asked her if she could let the child out of the cupboard. Jane replied with, "I can't". When asked why she couldn't, Jane responded that a voice had told her to kill the child and she was afraid that if she let him out of the cupboard, she would kill him.

The police officers reassured her that now that they were at the school, they would protect the child. They then helped Jane to her feet. She was escorted away from the classroom while the principal freed the child from the cupboard.[5]

3.6 Bipolar Disorder

How is bipolar disorder related to depression? Everyone at some point in their life experiences some degree of feeling down and, for that matter, euphoria as well. We all have down days and up days. But these mood swings are not necessarily indicative of a psychiatric condition. Nor do they necessarily indicate that treatment is required.

Bipolar disorder is characterised by the presence of simultaneous and/or rapidly alternating symptoms of depression **and** mania (see Appendix B for the criteria relating to a manic episode).

The most common form of bipolar disorder involves repeated episodes of mania and depression, usually separated by periods of complete remission or normal mood. **The person cycles between being really down and being really up** (i.e., "poles").

It used to be called manic-depressive illness, but now is typically called bipolar disorder.

Around 5-10% of individuals with clinical depression subsequently develop a manic episode, which may ultimately evolve into full-tilt bipolar disorder.

Bipolar disorder has a prevalence of 1-2% of the population.[5,6] While it is less common than clinical depression, bipolar symptoms suggest that the individual is much more likely to suffer severe functional impairment in the workplace, and **such dysfunction can have dire consequences for the workplace**.

We've already talked about the symptoms of depression, so what are the symptoms of a manic episode? They include the following:

1. **Elevated mood** (sometimes accompanied by irritability) which lasts for at least a week.

2. **Grandiosity or exaggerated self-esteem,** i.e., grandiose or huge ideas or a sense of being unstoppable. Heightened self-esteem can become grandiose to the point that it's delusional. For example, manics may believe they're qualified to advise prime ministers and presidents or capable of solving world hunger.

3. **Reduced need for sleep**. Manics often report feeling rested on very little sleep and have the energy to pursue many projects. In the early stages of mania, this heightened activity may be useful and goal-directed. In fact, manics who are only moderately ill can accomplish quite a lot in a twenty-hour day. However, as activity increases, agitation ensues, and they tend to start projects they will never complete.

4. **Increased talkativeness**, rapid speech, pressure to keep talking, and at times speech that is unintelligible. Manics are eager to tell anyone who will listen about their ideas, plans and work, and they tend to do so in loud, uninterruptible speech.

5. **Racing thoughts or flight of ideas,** in which one thought triggers another, to which it bears only a marginally logical association.

6. **Easily distracted or lack of concentration**, i.e., attention is too easily drawn to unimportant or irrelevant external stimuli.

7. **Increased energy** or increased goal-directed activity (such as social, school, or work activity).

8. **Increased libido,** often leading to a complete inhibition in public and inappropriate sexual activity (e.g., removing clothes in public, promiscuity). They are usually unaware that their behaviour is inappropriate.

A manic episode is represented by the elevated mood for **at least a week plus three or more of the other symptoms above.** The manic episode is sufficient to create disturbance in occupational functioning or in relationships with others.

Noted Johns Hopkins University School of Medicine Professor of Psychiatry, Kay Redfield Jamison, poignantly encapsulates the havoc created by her own bipolar illness, from the soaring manic episodes to crashing depression:

"I was a senior in high school when I had my first attack of manic-depressive illness. Once the siege began, I lost my mind rather rapidly. At first, everything seemed so easy. I raced about like a crazed weasel, bubbling with plans and enthusiasms, immersed in sports, and staying up all night, night after night, out with friends, reading everything that wasn't nailed down, filling manuscript books with poems and fragments of plays, and making expansive, completely unrealistic plans for my future.

The world was filled with pleasure and promise; I felt great. Not just great, I felt REALLY great. I felt I could do anything, that no task was too difficult.

My mind seemed clear, fabulously focused, and able to make intuitive mathematical leaps that had up to that point entirely eluded me. Indeed, they elude me still. At the time, however, not only did everything make perfect sense, but it all began to fit into a marvellous kind of cosmic relatedness.

My sense of enchantment with the laws of the natural world caused me to fizz over, and I found myself buttonholing my friends to tell them how beautiful it all was. They were less than transfixed by my insights and webbings and beauties of the universe, although considerably impressed by how exhausting it was to be around my enthusiastic ramblings. You're talking too fast, Kay. Slow down, Kay. And those times when they didn't actually come out and say it, I still could see it in their eyes: For God's sake, Kay slow down.

I did, finally, slow down. In fact, I came to a grinding halt. Unlike the very severe manic episodes that came a few years later and escalated wildly and psychotically out of control, this first sustained wave of mild mania was a light, lovely tincture of true mania; like hundreds of subsequent periods of high enthusiasms, it was short-lived and quickly burned itself out.

Then the bottom began to fall out of my life and mind. My thinking, far from being clearer than a crystal, was tortuous. I would read the same passage over and over again, only to realize that I had no memory of it at all.

Each book or poem I picked up was the same way. Incomprehensible. Nothing made sense. I could not begin to follow the material presented in my classes, and I would find myself staring out the window with no idea of what was going on around me. It was very frightening.

I was used to my mind being my best friend. Now all of a sudden, my mind had turned on me; it mocked me for my vapid enthusiasms; it laughed at all my foolish plans; it no longer found anything interesting or enjoyable or worthwhile. It was incapable of concentrated thought and turned time and again to the subject of death: I was going to die, what difference did anything make? Life's run was only a short and meaningless one, why live?

I was totally exhausted and could scarcely pull myself out of bed in the mornings. It took me twice as long to walk anywhere as it ordinarily did, and I wore the same clothes over and over again, as it was otherwise too much of an effort to make a decision about what to put on. I dreaded having to talk to people, avoided my friends whenever possible, and sat in the school library in the early mornings and late afternoons, virtually inert, with a dead heart and a brain as cold as clay."

Kay Redfield Jamison, *An Unquiet Mind*, 1995[7].

3.7 The Features of Bipolar Disorder at Work

We have already talked about the way that you can identify depression in the workplace, but what about the other end of the spectrum, the manic end? Well, you can probably deduce from the list above that certain features would show themselves more readily than others. Take the following:

1. **Elevated mood.** The employee may give the impression of being in really good shape and on top of the world, all the time. Life is grand. They are euphoric and over the top. On the other hand, some people who are manic experience intense anxiety and irritability, often to the point of rage. The elevated mood will be evident for at least a week or more.

2. **Grandiosity or exaggerated self-esteem,** i.e., grandiose or huge ideas or a sense of being unstoppable. Heightened self-esteem can become grandiose to the point that it's delusional. The world revolves around them. They can single-handedly turn around the company, or better still, turn the country's economy around.

3. **Goal directed**. Someone experiencing mania seems to have an enormous capacity for accomplishing work deadlines or work outputs. They may also be able to juggle a large number of jobs or tasks all at once. While this might be pleasing to management in the short-term, the perceptive leader will soon realise that "it ain't natural". One hint is when the employee mentions that they don't need much sleep, but they still have the energy to pursue many projects. Another tell-tale hint is that they start projects that they don't complete.

4. **Speech may be pressured or intense,** with a display of racing thoughts. Manics are eager to tell anyone who will listen about their ideas, plans and work, and they tend to do so in loud, often uninterruptible speech. People start to avoid them.

5. **Racing thoughts or flight of ideas.** They may exhibit flight of ideas, in which one thought triggers another, to which it bears only a marginally logical association or logical sequence. This makes them hard to follow and keep up with.

6. **Becomes distracted easily and lacks concentration**, i.e., their attention is too easily drawn to unimportant or trivial external stimuli. They find it difficult to stay on task.

7. **Increased energy** or increased goal-directed activity. They volunteer for numerous projects and committees. They work back, work on weekends, take work home and their emails are sent very late at night or very early morning.

8. **Increased libido,** often leading to inappropriate sexual activity or sexual harassment and promiscuity. They are not always aware that their behaviour is inappropriate.

9. **Impaired or poor judgment, and decision-making that leads to impulsive behaviour,** including gross overspending, spending sprees, or bad business investments. Manics often deny that anything is wrong, rationalising that no one who feels so good and so productive could possibly be ill. But they tend to ultimately wreak havoc on the lives of all who associate with them, and can wreak havoc in the workplace.

10. **Increased creativity**. This is often due to a combination of factors such as racing thoughts, lack of concentration and increased energy. Hence, there can be a demonstration of creative ideas and notions.

11. **Increased sociability** (wanting to meet and greet, and participate in lots of social activity). Manics often feel euphoric and may share their jolliness with others. Their humour may be quite infectious, but as the mania worsens, their humour becomes less cheerful. It begins to take on a driven, unfunny quality that makes others feel uncomfortable.

Chapter 3 Summary

It is true that depression takes many forms, but one is assured that it is a mental illness. According to the National Institute of Mental Health, a depressive disorder is "an illness that involves the body, mood, and thoughts. It affects the way a person eats and sleeps, the way one feels about oneself and the way one thinks about things".

According to the model put forward by Professor Gordon Parker,[3] there are **three categories** of clinical depressive disorders beyond the normal mood swings or normal depression that most of us feel with the general "ups and downs" of life.

Non-melancholic depression accounts for most of the people (90%) who are diagnosed with depression. It is usually activated by various life stressors which, in combination with the person's temperament and personality, means that they become depressed. It manifests through a combination of symptoms that interfere with the ability to work, study, sleep, eat, and enjoy once-pleasurable activities. Almost three-quarters of those who report clinical depression are in the labour force.

Melancholic depression is generally more severe than non-melancholic depression and accounts for about 5-10% of those diagnosed. In this category, though, there is evidence of psychomotor disturbance, in which the individual's movements are either retarded (e.g., speech is slow) or agitated (e.g., can't sit still) or both. The origins are primarily biological and/or genetic.

Psychotic melancholia is an extremely severe form of depression and accounts for only about 1-2% of those diagnosed with depression. It not only involves psychomotor disturbance, but includes delusions and hallucinations. It is thought to originate from disruptions in neural circuits and brain neurochemistry.

Bipolar disorder, also known as manic-depressive illness, is not as prevalent as other forms of depressive disorders, and is characterised by cycling mood changes – severe highs (mania) and severe lows (depression).

Irrespective of the label, managers and employees alike need to be alert to the symptoms that may be indicative of these disorders.

Make no mistake about it, people in your workplace right now have a depressive disorder of some kind.

Now that we have a sense of what depression might look like and the kinds of symptoms associated with depression, we can ask the critical questions: Who might be at risk, and what causes depression?

"Depression is the inability to construct a future."

Rollo May, 1909 - 1994
American existential psychologist

CHAPTER 4

Who Is At Risk?

Introduction

Who's at risk? The short answer; everyone. All of us. Each of us. No one is immune. Depression can happen to a person of any gender, age, race or social class.

However, as we have seen in Chapter 1, it does tend to be a more "western" phenomena and it does help if you have the genes on your side (see Chapter 5) and have developed some foundational resilience to your character (see also Chapter 5).

4.1 Who Is At Risk For Depression?

There are a number of theories about causes. The possible causes include the following:

1. Genetic factors

Depression seems to run in families. Research reveals that some people have a set of genes that makes them more likely, or pre-disposed, to develop a depressive episode or disorder. Depression is 1.5 to 3 times more common in biological relatives of persons with the disorder than in the general population.[1]

2. Chemical imbalance

Other research suggests that a chemical imbalance in the brain causes depression. Although the balance might be right most of the time, at other times the balance is altered and the person becomes depressed.

3. Stressful life events

As has been mooted above in Chapters 2 and 3, life "happens", and stressful events can play a part in the onset of depression. For example, on-going conflicts, either at work or at home, can sap our energy and take their toll, along with other stressors such as financial hardship, loneliness, relationship breakdown, retirement, unemployment, childbirth, the death of a spouse or friend, or the loss of something significant, like the home or a career.

Studies in Canada show that chronic workplace stress, whether real or imagined, is linked to higher odds for clinical depression. Particularly at risk are individuals whose jobs are highly skilled or involve constant new learning, who experience conflicting demands of job insecurity, who have unsupportive supervisors or co-workers, or who work evening and night shifts rather than regular hours.[2]

4. Personality factors

You've heard about the cup being half full versus the cup being half empty. Many people have a pessimistic outlook or view of life, and see everything in a negative light. Depression is more common among individuals who are less resilient, or who have not developed strong coping skills and have a sense of being overwhelmed, impotent or powerless. They are therefore more at risk for developing a depressive disorder.

5. Physical Illness or Disability

Depression and chronic physical health problems often go hand-in-hand. Interestingly, the annual prevalence of depression rises from 6% among pain-free individuals to over 25% among those with severe pain. In relation to pain, it's back pain that is most strongly linked to depression.[2]

Glandular fever, chronic fatigue syndrome, arthritis, diabetes, thyroid problems and cancer may all cause depression.

Further, younger people afflicted with chronic problems are more likely to become depressed than their elders. This is probably due to the fact that younger people have more to lose, and can be devastated by such diagnoses.

In short, although there are a number of theories, it seems reasonable to suggest that depression is a genetic and biological disorder that is exacerbated by stressful life events and a specific personality style.

In general, individuals who have experienced any of the following are at higher risk for clinical depression:
- A previous depressive episode (see Chapter 3, section 3.2)
- A family history of depression

- A difficult childhood, especially with physical, sexual or emotional abuse
- A substance abuse problem
- Being single, with no significant other person to relate to or connect with
- A recent bereavement
- Women who have recently given birth
- Recent serious medical conditions, such as stroke, heart attack(s) or diabetes, or injuries such as back complaints and shoulder or arm restrictions
- A recent life-altering trauma, such as military service or witnessing a fatal accident
- Recent severe stressors, such as divorce or loss of employment

Additionally, women are at significantly greater risk than men to develop major depressive episodes at some point in their lives. Studies also show that depressive episodes occur twice as frequently in women as in men.[1]

4.2 The Incidence and Prevalence of Depression

Clinical depression plagues every population across the globe. It is no respecter of persons. And no respecter of workplaces. Mood disorders, like depression, in conjunction with other mental illnesses, account for more than 40% of workforce losses each year, making them the second most common disability worldwide.[3]

To get a true picture of depression's grasp on the population, it's important to distinguish between the terms **"incidence"** and **"prevalence"** as they're applied to statistics related to disorders and diseases.

Incidence refers to the annual diagnosis rate, or the number of new cases of depression. **Prevalence** refers to the number of people who are managing depression at any given time.

For example, a short-lived disease like flu might have high annual incidence, but low prevalence. Many new cases of flu are reported each year, but for most people, flu will not prevail; they will recover quickly. A chronic disease like diabetes, however, has a lower annual incidence, but high prevalence, since diabetes isn't curable and must be managed on an ongoing basis. Unfortunately, depression also prevails for many.

The following statistics paint a portrait of both the **incidence and prevalence** of depression across the globe:

- Severe clinical depression is associated with high mortality. As we have already seen, up to 15% of those suffering from major clinical depression will die by suicide, and recent evidence suggests a fourfold risk increase in people over 55 years of age. [1]

- Mental disorders are the leading cause of disability in the U.S. and Canada for people aged 15 to 44 years. [4]

- A well-known study conducted by Harvard University and the National Mental Institute of Health predicted that by 2020 (and that of course, was before the covid-19 pandemic), depression would be second only to heart disease as the leading cause of disability and death, and would account for 15% of the disease burden in the world. [5]

- An estimated 5.8% of men and 9.5% of women worldwide will experience a depressive episode in any given year. [4]

- At any given time, nearly one in ten people is experiencing symptoms of severe depression in the U.S. population.[3]

- 10-25% of women and 5-12% of men will become clinically depressed and experience a major depressive episode or develop clinical depression at some point in their lives.[1]

- Between 8-12% of the U.K. population experiences depression in any given year.[6]

- In Australia, 5.8% of all adults suffer from a depressive disorder each year. Depressive disorders affect 7.4% of females and 4.2% of males annually.[7]

- In Canada, 10-12% of adults will have clinical depression during their lifetime.[7]

Depression takes a monumental toll in human suffering, lost productivity and suicide. As has already been mooted, depression is currently estimated to cause the largest amount of non-fatal health burden worldwide, accounting for 12% of total years lived with disability.[9] In other words, more people are living with depression than any other non-fatal illness. We can live with depression, but we do not live with it unharmed. And it always follows us to work.

When contemplating how to respond to depression in the workplace, organisations must never lose sight of the fact that clinical depression is associated with high mortality. Tragically, depression, for many, is a life-threatening illness, and for some, a killer.

4.3 Gender and Cultural Differences

Are the distinctive qualities of each individual's depression determined by biological differences between men and women...between the very young and the very old...between Asians and Europeans...or are they determined more by what we call sociological differences? In other words, are any differences due to the expectations that society imposes on people according to the population they happen to live in or represent?

The answer in every case, is both. Depression is always contextual, and must be interpreted within the context in which it occurs.

Let's look at some of the factors that can trigger depression in various populations.

4.3.1 Gender

Men and women often experience depression differently, and each gender has different coping mechanisms. As we've seen already, at some stage in their lives, 10-25% of women become clinically depressed in comparison to 5-12% of men. In general, men tend to externalise symptoms, whereas women tend to internalise symptoms. Let's look at that further.

"When women are depressed, they eat or go shopping. Men invade another country. It's a whole different way of thinking."

Elayne Boosler, 1952-
American comedian

4.3.1.1 The Male Experience

How do men experience depression? Males tend to mask their pain and resort to self-defeating ways of managing their emotions. It's the "be strong" syndrome which many men grow up with – the message is that "Big boys don't cry". Men typically hide their real feelings.

However, those feelings have to come out somewhere. Hence, men are more likely than women to engage in destructive, often addictive behaviours when they're depressed, such as turning to alcohol or drugs, or becoming frustrated, discouraged, irritable, angry, or even abusive or violent.

Many men have trouble managing anger. Spouses and workmates often give gratuitous advice, such as, "You shouldn't be angry", or "You should always be nice no matter what", or "You should try to please people", or, "If you get angry, people won't like you". Men naturally bite back at their annoyance, their irritations and their anger, until they can't take it anymore, and boom – they can explode. They may even neglect or abuse spouses and children. This is more likely if there has been some prior abuse in their family of origin; the role model of abuse is, unfortunately, a powerful teacher.

Many walk around with a vast hurt inside and a longing for someone to heal it. But they're also ashamed of those feelings, so they don't let anyone know. Remember, "Big boys don't cry", and besides, you don't want to appear to be a "wimp" or to be weak somehow. Always expecting rejection in some form, or feeling that they may not be good enough, men may reject others as a first defence. The hurt, in other words, makes them defensive and hard to get along with.

Some men become workaholics to avoid thinking about their depression and discussing how they feel with family or friends. Work is a good distraction (and usually, a socially accepted one). Others engage in reckless, risky behaviour, such as engaging in illicit love affairs. If, for whatever reason, a man does confront behaviour such as over-working or drinking too much, it is then that the depression may emerge.

Rather than acknowledging feelings, instead, men are more likely to acknowledge being fatigued, being irritable, losing interest in once-pleasurable activities (e.g., sports, sex, hobbies), and experiencing sleep disturbances.

Even though more women attempt suicide, many more men actually complete suicide. In fact, almost four times as many males as females die by suicide.[10] Typically, clinical experience shows that women often commit suicide as a result of a relationship breakdown, or if they have been emotionally disconnected from someone special or significant in their lives. On the other hand, men typically commit suicide because they have a lack of purpose in their lives, they lack goals, or they cannot find a solution to a problem and they feel overwhelmed or feel like a failure. That typifies the difference between the sexes.

"When I was diagnosed, I was incensed. 'I am not depressed', I said to my doctor, 'I'm just a bit stressed and run down, that's all'. To be frank, I was suppressing everything because I couldn't bare to think that I was emotionally unbalanced somehow. I was very defensive and angry. In hindsight, I now realise that I was not well at all.

Depression undermines who you are and what you are about.

Your ability to think and reason is stripped away. There is no escape from knowing that something is wrong. I couldn't sleep properly and I was constantly tired with no energy. I even woke up feeling tired. And my exhaustion made everything worse.

I tried to hide the problem at work for a good period of time, but I came to a point where I just couldn't go on. I'm not sure what brought me to that point at that particular time, but I just couldn't go on any longer. I must admit that at that point, I started to panic.

Thankfully, I could take time off and I had a supportive workplace and wonderful support from my family. When I finally fell in a hole at work, I had to go to the doctor. I'm so grateful now that the doctor was able to pick the problem and that my work and family rallied around me. I'm not sure where I'd be if that hadn't have happened."

4.3.1.2 The Female Experience

How do women experience depression? Women are more likely than men to admit to feelings of sadness, worthlessness and excessive guilt – all hallmarks of depression. That's one reason why they are more likely to visit their local doctor; they are generally more in touch with their feelings, more self-aware.

Women though, are more prone than men to becoming trapped in a cycle of despair, helplessness and passivity. This seems to be particularly true of women who perceive that they have less social power than men and less control over important areas of their lives, such as their careers or their money.

Women report feeling unappreciated by their partners more often than men do. In addition to workplace stress, a woman may bear a greater burden for housework and childcare than does a man. Some women must also cope with the additional stresses of caring for aging parents, abuse, poverty, or relationship problems. They feel stretched in all directions. It's like there's not enough of them to go around.

Research has shown that this sense of powerlessness and the "grinding annoyances and burdens that come with women's lower social power", causes chronic stress.[10] Chronic stress provokes chronic rumination – the churning of feelings over and over again as the self-talk goes round and round in one's head like a never-ending whirlpool.

Rumination can help perpetuate chronic stress because it depletes the reservoir of motivation, perseverance, and problem-solving skills that is required to facilitate positive change. Chronic rumination provokes more chronic stress. You can see that this is a vicious cycle.

Women between the ages of 18 and 45 comprise the majority of those with clinical depression.[5] In the U.S., for example, clinical depression is twice as common in adolescent and adult females as in adolescent and adult males.[1] This increased differential highlights that depression in women often coincides with the onset of puberty.

While biology alone does not account for the high rate of women's depression, biological, life cycle, hormonal and psychosocial factors unique to women are linked to women's higher depression rates. Researchers have shown that hormones directly affect the brain chemistry that controls emotions and mood. For example, many women report worsening of depressive symptoms several days before the onset of menstruation. Some women are susceptible to a severe form of premenstrual syndrome (PMS), sometimes called premenstrual dysphoric disorder (PMDD), due to hormonal changes that typically occur around ovulation. In fact, many scientists believe that the cyclical rise and fall of estrogen and other hormones may affect the brain chemistry that is associated with depression. Some women experience an increased risk for depression during the transition into menopause.[5]

Childbirth. Becoming a parent is one of the most significant life-changing events a person ever experiences. Just ask any parent! Women are particularly vulnerable to depression after giving birth, when hormonal and physical changes – added to the new responsibility of caring for a newborn – can be overwhelming.

Following the birth of a baby, up to 80% of new mothers experience a brief episode of the "baby blues". Generally, the baby blues is a transient condition that occurs within 3-10 days following childbirth, and if the woman has a strong emotional support system, the baby blues will vanish.

Childbirth, however, can precipitate a major depressive episode, both before and after delivery of the baby. Some women experience depression during pregnancy, known as antenatal depression. In Australia, for example, antenatal depression affects 10% of all pregnant women.[11]

Some women develop postpartum depression (PPD), also called post-natal depression (PND), a much more serious depressive condition for which active treatment and emotional support are required. PND occurs one month to one year following the birth of the baby, and can develop gradually or suddenly. It affects 16% of the women in Australia, for instance, who give birth. This post-natal depression may delay a return to the workplace. Once a woman returns after maternity leave, it is possible that she may still be depressed.

> *"At first I thought what I was feeling was just exhaustion, but with it came an overriding sense of panic that I had never felt before. Rowan kept crying and I suddenly began to fear the moment when Chris would bring her back to me.*
>
> *I started to experience a sick sensation in my stomach; it was as if a vice was tightening around my chest. Instead of the nervous anxiety that accompanies panic, a feeling of quiet devastation overcame me. I hardly moved. Sitting on my bed, I let out a deep, slow guttural wail. I wasn't simply emotional or weepy like I had been told I might be. This was something different. This was sadness of a shockingly different magnitude. It felt as if it would never go away."*
>
> Brooke Shields, *Down Came the Rain: A Mother's Story of Depression and Recovery*, 2005.

4.3.2 Race and Ethnicity

Interestingly, the employer or manager needs to also be aware that different cultures may allude to depression in different ways. In assessing an employee, it's important not to dismiss or misinterpret a potential depressive symptom merely because it is not the norm for one's own culture.

Culture can influence both the symptoms of depression and the way those symptoms are experienced and communicated.

In some cultures, depression may be experienced largely in somatic or physical terms, rather than in terms of feelings such as sadness or guilt.

For instance, Latino and Mediterranean cultures may refer to complaints of "nerves" and headaches; Asian and Chinese cultures may refer to weakness, tiredness or "imbalance"; and Middle Eastern cultures can refer to it as problems of the heart. The Hopi people who live in north-eastern Arizona may express the depressive experience as being heartbroken.

"I cry a lot. My emotions are very close to the surface. I don't want to hold anything in so it festers and turns into pus – a pustule of emotion that explodes into a festering cesspool of depression."

Nicolas Cage, 1964-
American Actor, Producer and Film Director

Chapter 4 Summary

Depression is estimated to cause the largest amount of non-fatal health burden worldwide. Populations that are at high risk for depression include those with a family history of depression, those with a substance abuse problem, and those who have experienced a recent severe stressor or previous depressive episode. Women are at significantly greater risk for depression than men, especially women who have recently given birth.

Each individual's depression is *individual*, and must be interpreted in the context of many factors such as gender and ethnicity. Men and women, for example, tend to experience depression differently, and their symptoms may manifest differently. In general, men tend to externalise symptoms, whereas women tend to internalise symptoms.

Culture and ethnicity can also influence the way an individual experiences depression, as well as the way their symptoms are interpreted by others. In some cultures, a person may communicate depressive symptoms in somatic terms rather than in terms of feelings.

There's a lot for a manager or leader in the workplace to think about, let alone being aware of the individuality of depression. Suffice it to say that sometime soon in your career, chances are you will encounter a depressed staff member or employee (if you haven't already), and simply remembering the nine symptoms listed in Chapter 3 is an important step, along with remembering that men and women are different (surprise, surprise), and that different cultures may present or talk about depression differently.

CHAPTER 5

What Causes Depression?

Introduction

Depression is not a monolith. Its aetiology, or causes, vary from person to person, and, in fact, it can be caused by a combination of factors in any one individual.

The forces contributing to a person's depression may include biological or genetic factors, past history (including upbringing, childhood loss and trauma), personality and psychological maturity factors (such as whether or not the person has well-developed coping skills), external circumstances (such as work or finances), and social relationships (including social discord, parenting demands and social isolation).

All these factors can effect a person in various ways and impact their thoughts, feelings and physiology, and, of course, their behaviour and how they act. Figure 5.1 on the next page shows a diagram of the factors which bring about depression.

Figure 5.1

Causes & Effects of Depression

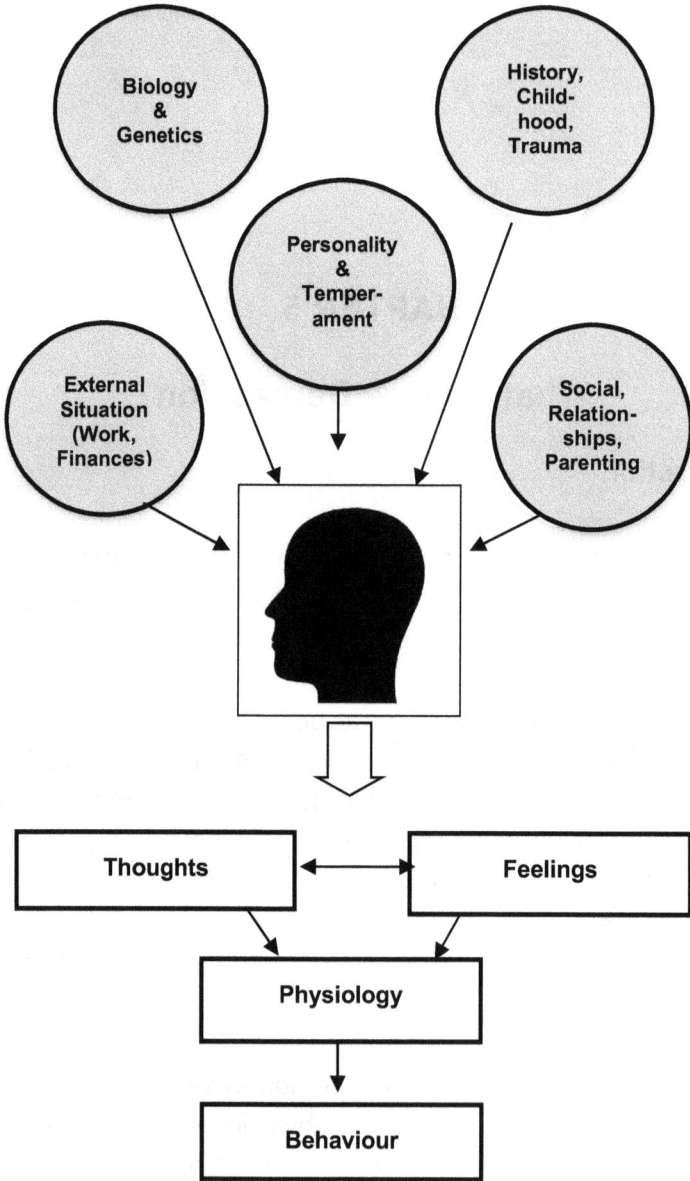

No two people have the same depression. In *Noonday Demon*, author Andrew Solomon encapsulates the varying faces of depression like this: "Like snowflakes, depressions are always unique, each based on the same essential principles, but each boasting an irreproducibility complex shape".[1]

But one thing is for sure: depression signals, first and foremost, that certain mental and emotional aspects of a person's life are out of balance.

Let's look more closely at some known causes of depression.

5.1 Biology and Genetics

5.1.1 Genetics

Can you be born into the wrong family? In other words, is there a genetic link to depression? You'll often hear the expression, "Depression runs in families". Is this true?

Studies done with twins who have the same set of genes show that if one twin has a depressive disorder, there is a 70% chance that the other twin will also develop a depressive disorder. In contrast, with non-twin brothers and sisters whose genes are not exactly the same, there is only a 15% chance that one will develop a depressive disorder if the other sibling has such a disorder.[2]

The conclusion is that some people seem to have a set of genes that make them more likely to develop a depressive disorder, though scientists, so far, have not specifically identified a depression gene.

5.1.2 Brain Chemicals: Neurotransmitters

One theory for the cause of depression is that it involves an incorrect balance of chemicals in the brain. Although the balance may be right most of the time, at other times, the balance may change, and the person becomes depressed.

Changes in brain chemistry influence mood and thought processes. Depression is believed to result from changes in brain chemicals, specifically the neurotransmitters. Neurotransmitters act as chemical messengers that send messages from one nerve cell to another, allowing communication between the brain and the rest of the body. There are many different neurotransmitters in the brain of which about 100 have been identified. Of these, three are of particular importance with mood regulation.

The most well-known is **serotonin**. During depression, quantities of the neurotransmitter serotonin, in particular, are significantly reduced. Serotonin promotes social confidence and a feeling of well-being. If serotonin levels are high, your confidence soars and you feel less vulnerable. If serotonin levels are low, you may feel helpless, and become defensive and less willing to take risks.

Serotonin also plays a key role in maintaining a proper perspective on events. For example, serotonin modulates rejection sensitivity. Lower serotonin levels can cause depressed people to be acutely sensitive to rejection.[3]

Noradrenaline is the second neurotransmitter important to mood regulation. It is generally known for its role in the "fight or flight" response, in which it puts the brain and body on red alert in the face of danger, so that the individual can either defend or escape. It therefore regulates arousal, the cardiovascular system, and primes the brain for alarm signals in the environment. Noradrenaline also acts as a regulator of other neurotransmitters such as serotonin, and hence is considered to play a role both directly and indirectly in regulating mood state.

Dopamine is the third neurotransmitter which regulates mood. It is found in a range of locations across the brain and is involved in a variety of processes including reward, emotion and movement.

It has been known for more than fifty years that these three principal neurotransmitters play a role in regulating mood. This has been demonstrated repeatedly through experiments in animals and the successful use of anti-depressants in humans.[4]

Especially over the last decade, all types of depression have been equated to a lack of serotonin or disruption in its neurotransmission. This is directly reflected in the development of anti-depressants that act selectively on serotonin alone, called "selective serotonin reuptake inhibitors", or SSLIs. Anti-depressants having specific noradrenaline or dopamine actions are far fewer and have only recently been developed and made available.

5.1.3 Stress Hormone: Cortisol

Cortisol is a stress hormone that can provoke depressed moods. In depressed people, cortisol is produced in excess, and is responsible for much of the physiological damage caused by long-term stress.

Depressives often aren't aware of what triggered their depression. Why is this? When a memory or live event triggers depression, feeling is separated from thought. The depressive loses the thought, but the feeling keeps on churning. This is why you'll often hear depressives say, "It just came out of the blue", when, in fact, depression never "comes out of the blue".

Here's how this psychological discontinuity happens neurologically. The conscious, second-by-second processing of verbal conversation happens in one part of the brain – the prefrontal lobes of the neocortex – while your emotional evaluations are happening in another part of the brain – in the limbic system, which is a network of brain structures involved in learning, memory, motivation and generating emotions.

When you hear a stress-inducing statement, two things happen: (1) Your language and working memory centres decode the meaning and insert the meaning into the conscious mind; (2) A subcortical system triggers a stress response – your limbic system launches a cascade of events that sends chemicals, including cortisol, racing throughout your body. Terrorist attacks and economic recessions, for example, could spike cortisol surges.

The prefrontal lobe activity, which is the conscious, intelligent processing of the stress-inducing statement, happens in nanoseconds. However, the emotional system lags behind for seconds, even minutes, so there's still cortisol floating around in the bloodstream thirty seconds or more after the news vanishes from working memory, yet you no longer remember what triggered the depressed mood.

For example, you may hear of a co-worker being terminated or retrenched under circumstances that are eerily similar to those in which you were once terminated from a job. Even if you don't feel that your current job is endangered, you associate the memory of your past traumatic experience with your co-worker's plight, triggering a depressed mood.

5.1.4 Relevant Brain Structures

Do brain structures play a role in depression? The amygdala and the hippocampus are a pair of small brain structures that work in tandem to generate emotions, attach emotions to memories, and store and index those memories. Our minds are wonderful computers, aren't they?

The almond-shaped **amygdala** is located on the back of your brain stem, and is the brain's emotion factory – the "gut feeling" centre of the brain. It serves as the emotional traffic cop, to quickly determine what's safe and what's not. When people were hunters and gatherers, it worked to make sure that when they needed to run from danger, freeze or defend themselves, they quickly did so. The amygdala often tells you to do things (or to not do things) before the more advanced part of your brain, the neo-cortex, has a chance to examine the situation carefully and determine whether it's safe or not.

Located beside the amygdala is the **hippocampus**, a small brain structure shaped like a seahorse. The hippocampus is the brain's spatial memory bank – a memory map room that stores and keeps track of memories, much like the directory system on a hard drive. It is a specialised part of our memory bank, the contents of which are stored right next door to "emotion central", the amygdala. Some scientists believe that the amygdala is able to somehow mark memories created by other parts of the brain as being emotionally significant. Maybe this works a bit like bookmarks on your favourite web pages. The net impact is that our sense of place ties to our recollections of experiences and our sense of comfort or unease in the world.

Severe stress, however, gets in the way of our ability to form memories. Functional Magnetic Resonance Imaging (fMRI) studies have shown that the hippocampi of depressives are smaller than those of individuals with no history of depression. Why does this matter? A smaller hippocampus supports fewer feel-good serotonin receptors. A serotonin deficit, remember, can trigger depression.

Some researchers believe that depressed individuals may simply be born with a smaller hippocampus, which would predispose them to suffer from depression. Some believe that extended release of the stress hormone cortisol is toxic to the hippocampus' ability to form memories.[5]

Extended release of the other stress hormones, such as glucortocoid, actually cause hippocampus nerve cells to atrophy. During a traumatic event, for example, a person's stress response weakens the hippocampus so much that the memory never forms, even though the amygdala – emotion central – still manages to capture the essence of the traumatic event. The result is an incomplete emotional memory – a "flashbulb memory" – which may help explain why the specific traumatic memory has a tendency to disappear from consciousness while persisting in our gut reactions and phobias, and ultimately contributing to depression.

The good news, though, is that nerve cell atrophy in the hippocampus is reversible if the stress ends.

5.1.5 Complications of Other Medical Conditions

Up to 20-25% of individuals with general medical conditions such as diabetes, cancer, myocardial infarction (heart attack), carcinomas and stroke will develop severe clinical depression during the course of their medical condition. Further, depressives have been shown to have a high prevalence (65-71%) of the most common chronic medical conditions.[6]

Depression can also rear its ugly head when individuals suffer serious injuries, particularly when the injuries result in chronic pain, such as back pain. Depression intensifies pain and physical suffering. It causes fatigue and a decrease in energy that tends to worsen over time.

Common complications include:
- Problems with serious illnesses, e.g., heart disease, diabetes and cancer
- Exacerbated hypertension and arthritis
- Migraine headaches
- Severe backaches and abdominal or other pains
- Sexual dysfunction
- Sleep disorders

Naturally, when a person is clinically depressed, managing the medical condition becomes more complicated, and the long-term outlook is less favourable. By the same token, a serious medical condition adversely affects the prognosis of a person who has severe clinical depression. For example, a depressive who's juggling a serious medical condition is more likely to suffer longer depressive episodes and not respond as well to treatment, particularly when the medical condition is chronic. People suffering a chronic illness often have difficulty adjusting to the demands of the illness while focusing on treatment.

Chronic illness often affects a person's ability to get around and to be independent. It can also affect their self-identity – the way a person views themselves and relates to others. Ultimately, the onset of depression complicates medical conditions. While clinical depression may not cause the medical condition, it certainly makes it worse.

5.1.6 Depression and Immune Dysfunction

Severe, chronic stress depresses the immune function and, in turn, a reduced immune system diminishes the body's capacity to fight diseases and disorders. In other words, people suffering from chronic stress get more colds, flu and infections than do others.

Chronic or long-term activation of the body's stress response leads to what is called allostatic load, which is a prolonged wear-and-tear on the body. Allostatic load levels are high in depressed and anxious people. Their impact on the human body is similar to what happens to a car or appliance after years of wear and tear.

A high allostatic load level is associated with the following:
- Impaired immunity
- Accelerated atherosclerosis and increased incidence of type 2 diabetes
- Obesity
- Hypertension (high blood pressure)
- Hyperlipidemia (excess of fats in the blood)
- Bone demineralisation due to chronically high levels of havoc-wreaking cortisol and atrophy of nerve cells in the brain[7]

Depression occurs more frequently in those with immune disorders. A depleted immune system induces sickness behaviour such as apathy, lethargy, lack of motivation and appetite irregularities – all of which are symptoms of depression.[7]

5.2 History and Upbringing

In many ways, our past has a way of catching up with us. This is particularly so in relation to our childhood and upbringing.

Clinically, there are many cases of adults who cite a history of physical, sexual or emotional abuse as a child, and consider that it has impacted their lives, including leading to depression. Instability and insecurity during childhood can lead to a number of psychological disorders, including periods of depression.

Family dynamics are complex, especially when we throw into the mix blended families, broken families, separated families, stepmothers and stepfathers, step-siblings, half brothers and sisters, and so on.

As we grow up, the interactions resulting from these dynamics can lead to certain insecurities, meaning that we are more predisposed to a number of disorders, including depression.

"I can still recall how cruel my stepmother was when I was growing up. You know, it was like I could never do anything right. She would criticise me for all sorts of things and find fault – nothing was ever good enough. I did try for a while, but eventually I just gave up. She was a real bitch. I used to spend

hours in my room crying and later, when I was a teenager, I did all I could to be out of the house.

It was fine when she was dating dad, but once she came to live with us and then she married him, it was like she was the dragon from hell. She definitely favoured her own two kids and it seemed that I was really just a nuisance in her life. I used to cry to dad and tell him she was being really mean and nasty, but he would just shrug it off and say that I should maybe try harder to get on with her. In hindsight, I really don't think he knew what to do.

But I know that it affected me in my life and there are times, you know, when I think that I've never really gotten over it."

5.3 Personality and Temperament

5.3.1 Dependency on the Symbols of Success

It is sometimes said that you can't judge a book by its cover. Depressives often look good on the outside, but inside it's a different story. All that glitters is not gold.

Depressives have a leak in the part of the self that contains a positive self-image. They have no reliable reservoir of self-esteem. As a result, they're often overly dependent on love, respect, approval and recognition from others.

In fact, they're often dependent on constant positive feedback; they often like to look good, keep up appearances and be told that they look good. (Of course, some depressives, especially in severe cases, literally give up caring about their appearance.) On the other hand though, the non-depressive needs only periodic maintenance of self-esteem, and isn't thrown for a loop by being ignored or somehow overlooked. When depressives don't get the positive feedback or recognition they crave, depression escalates.

Sometimes this endless need is not obvious, and what's visible instead is a dependency on the *symbols* of love, respect and approval, e.g., financial success, control, power, and material possessions. In fact, depressives often chase the symbols of success to fill the void inside – the new car, the designer label clothes, the bigger house, or to be seen at the theatre on opening night, or at an art gallery opening. They may believe that, "I need to have the trappings of success in order to get the recognition that I need, because without that, I'm nothing".

5.3.2 Negative Thinking

In many cases, people have no control over the circumstances that trigger depression (e.g., retrenchment, financial loss). "Stuff happens", as they say.

"The optimist proclaims that we live in the best of all possible worlds; and the pessimist fears this is true."

James Cabell, 1879-1958
American author

For many people, when "stuff" does occur, they are simply unable to see that they have choices and can bring about change in their lives, or do something about the stuff. Of course, an external event like a death, accident or job loss can have some initial devastating effects on the individual. It's natural to feel numb, angry, anxious, guilty or depressed. But staying in a depressed mood for an extended period of time (i.e. more than two weeks), is not healthy. You often can't dictate whether the cup is half empty or half full, but you can decide how you will *think* about the cup.

Psychotherapists generally agree that the impact of a particular stressor is moderated by the personal meaning of the event or situation. Cognitive theories of depression in particular, emphasise that **how we perceive and interpret stressful events** helps determine whether or not those events will trigger depression.

For example, a romantic breakup will trigger a much stronger emotional response if the affected person has thoughts such as, "I am empty and incomplete without her love", or, "I will never find another who makes me feel the way he does". Similarly, a job demotion or loss of employment can evoke strong emotional responses if the person's self-talk is something like, "I'll never find another job like this one", or, "My life is ruined", or "I'm all washed up, a has-been".

"An optimist sees an opportunity in every calamity; a pessimist sees a calamity in every opportunity."

Winston Churchill, 1874-1965
Prime Minister of the United Kingdom

Real pessimists, or "worry-warts", as they often call themselves, tend to have highly irrational or faulty thought patterns. For example, they tend to accentuate the following:

1. **Global Impact:** *This event will have a big effect on me ("This is the end, I'm ruined.")*

2. **Internality:** *I should have done something to prevent this ("I knew I really wasn't good enough for this job – it's all my fault.")*

3. **Irreversibility:** *I'll never be able to recover from this ("I'll never get over losing this job.")*

Negative self-talk often stems from listening to and learning from our parent(s). You often hear people say things like, "I'm a worrier, just like my mother", or "I stress out just like the ol' man". Negative thinking can also be activated by stressful, adverse life events, particularly when a person is in a down mood ("I never get any good breaks", or "That kind of thing always happens to me", or "If it had to go wrong, I'd be the one".)

Ways out of this kind of negative spiral can be found in the book that I have written titled, *Stopping Your Self-sabotage: Steps to Increase Your Self-confidence,* which can be found under the Resources tab at www.drdarryl.com. Alternatively, you can go direct to https://howtostopselfsabotage.com .

Prolonged negative thinking can become an endless negative feedback loop, in which one negative thought feeds another and another and another. Soon the person is ensnared in a downward spiral that can lead to full-tilt clinical depression.

"For as long as I can remember, I used to worry a lot and would beat up on myself with my internal head talks. I used to wish that I could switch off all my thoughts with my head going round and round – most of it negative all the time.

Then when the company went under and we were all laid off, I thought it was the end for me. I got really depressed and used to just sit at home. My wife got really concerned for me and demanded that I go and see our doctor. I couldn't be bothered at first, but she insisted, so I decided to go.

He diagnosed me with depression and gave me some medication, and also wrote out a referral to go and see a psychologist. He said it would help to talk about it and he said that the psychologist could give me some hints on how to stop my thoughts always being negative.

The psychologist helped, and one of the things he told me was what one of the early philosophers once said: "It's not the things of this world that hurt us, but it's the way that we think about them". That got me thinking. Now I'm trying to think more positively.

5.3.3 Lack of Coping Skills and Resilience

Why do some people become depressed when confronted by stress or trauma, and others don't? The answer may be their lack of psychological resilience. Resilience is the ability to bounce back and not feel overwhelmed, which brings on anxiety and depression.

Examples of famous resilient people, such as Anne Frank and Helen Keller, easily come to mind. But resilience can be seen in ordinary people on any ordinary day. One of the keys to resilience is developing effective coping skills. Coping strategies may involve problem-solving skills, internal emotional skills, and inner confidence, as well as social support from others.

What are the characteristics of a resilient person?
- Can cope with grief and anxiety
- Bounces back and recovers from almost anything, including traumatic experiences
- Is optimistic, takes chances and embraces life, as opposed to engaging in harsh self-criticisms and holding negative self-images
- Has a "where there's a will, there's a way" attitude
- Has a tendency to view problems as opportunities or challenges, and make the most of those opportunities
- Has a deep-rooted spiritual or philosophical faith
- Has a healthy social support network
- Maintains good physical health
- Has an ability to adapt and competently handle a wide variety of problems
- Has an ability to persevere and navigate through the fall-out after a crisis
- Possesses strong self-efficacy, i.e. has confidence in their own ability to cope with adversity, whether independently or with assistance from others

Resilience is a dynamic quality, not a permanent capacity. The less resilient frequently find themselves worn down and negatively impacted by life's stresses. The truly resilient have learned the art of self-renewal. Resilient individuals not only cope well with severe stressors, but actually experience challenges as learning and development opportunities.

5.4 External Situations and Circumstances

5.4.1 Psychosocial Stressors

Psychosocial stressors are stress-triggering events that impact various aspects of a person's social and psychological behaviour. Clinical depression can be triggered by what is called a severe psychosocial stressor. Most of us know about these kinds of events or we know others who have had bad stuff happen in their lives.

What would you say are the most common stressors in our lives? The National Institute for Mental Health in the U.S. lists the following: [6]

- Death of a family member or friend
- Economic hardships
- Racism and discrimination
- Poor physical health
- Assaults on physical safety

However, other more subtle factors that impact a person's sense of identity or self-esteem may contribute to depression, for example, a job demotion, or a spouse who constantly belittles and criticises.

Normal, but significant life transitions can also trigger depression. Examples might include:

- Moving one's residence or place of living
- Graduating from school, training college or university
- Changing jobs or losing a job

- Getting married or divorced
- Retiring from a career

Studies suggest that psychosocial stressors play a more significant role in triggering the first and second major depressive episodes, but less of a role in the onset of subsequent episodes.[3]

5.4.2 Traumatic Events

It just comes out of the blue. You are not expecting it. You are driving to work like you have done for years and suddenly you are involved in a major vehicular accident. It's not just unsettling, it's traumatic, because it threatens life and limb, and is quite out of the ordinary and sudden.

A life-threatening event (e.g., a fire at home, bomb threat, robbery, hold-up, accident or "near miss" at work, or a physical or verbal assault) frequently provokes emotional and behavioural reactions that jeopardise mental health. In the most fully-developed form, this syndrome is called post-traumatic stress disorder, or PTSD. Women are twice as likely as men to develop PTSD following life-threatening traumas.[3]

Such a dramatic event shakes the foundation of our beliefs about safety and shatters our assumptions of trust. We may be involved directly in the trauma or we may simply witness it (e.g., a bank robbery, a car accident). Irrespective, the traumatic situation is often described as "terrifying" or "a nightmare", and the individual has extreme difficulty being able to get back to a normal way of living again. Not surprisingly, many people can point to a traumatic event as the source of their depressive episode.

5.4.3 Depression Often Co-occurs with Other Psychological Disorders

Depression may be caused by, or co-occur (known as comorbidity) with other psychological disorders. The following disorders often co-occur with clinical depression:

Bipolar disorders. Depressive episodes cycled with manic episodes is characteristic of bipolar disorders, i.e. large mood swings up and down as we have already discussed in Chapter 3.

Personality disorders. Depressed mood is almost invariably a part of a borderline personality disorder, but can accompany other personality disorders, such as avoidant, dependent, or histrionic (i.e. attention-seeking, volatile, or emotional) personality disorders.

Substance-induced mood disorders. Nearly 30% of individuals who have substance abuse problems also suffer from clinical depression. Alcohol and other substances can cause depressed mood, as well as the elevated mood associated with manic episodes.

Schizoaffective disorders. Symptoms of schizophrenia often coexist with major depressive or manic episodes.

Cognitive disorders. Depression often coexists with cognitive disorders such as dementia or Alzheimer's disease. Delirium can often begin with depression or anxiety.

Adjustment disorders. These individuals are generally tearful, sad, hopeless, and have difficulty adapting to life's stressors.

Other disorders. Depression accompanies a broad range of other disorders, including eating disorders, sexual and gender identity disorders, panic disorder, obsessive-compulsive disorder, phobic disorder, post-traumatic stress disorder, and somatisation disorder.

5.5 Social Relationships

5.5.1 Bereavement and Loss

Few losses in life can compare to the death of a loved one. The death of a child or spouse during early or mid-adult life is far less common than divorce, but generally is a far more powerful depression trigger.[6]

Unfortunately, people are unlikely to seek professional treatment during bereavement, unless the severity of the emotional and behavioural disturbance is somehow overwhelming or incapacitating.

Common symptoms associated with bereavement include crying spells, appetite changes, weight loss, sleep disturbances, poor concentration, and ruminations on sad thoughts and feelings – symptoms common to clinical depression.

Bereaved individuals may also suffer unwarranted guilt, believing that somehow they could have prevented the death. Grief, of course, typically has a severe emotional impact, but is not diagnosed as a depressive disorder unless there are clear complications, such as incapacity, psychosis or suicidal thoughts.

5.5.2 Breakdown of Support Networks

Until recently, humans maintained a network of extended family around them, including aunts, uncles, cousins and grandparents where we all lived in a community or nearby. We all backed each other up and helped out in times of need.

Today all that has changed. Our family members may be on the other side of the country or the other side of the world. We lack the support and back-up that we had in times past. No-one there who can just drop in and lend a hand, have a chat or provide a shoulder to cry on.

The nuclear family can split even further when parents separate or divorce, taking extended family and friends far away. Hence, we feel isolated and lost. We feel unsupported and overwhelmed. We often feel depressed.

5.5.3 The Role of Parenting

Just ask any parent about how difficult parenting really is. Somehow or other, we are supposed to be "good" at it when there are no real training courses, and no manuals that arrived with the birth of the baby! To make matters worse, everyone seems to have advice on how to do it and there are a babble of voices and 'experts'. I have written about this in an earlier book titled, *"Growing Up Children: How to Get 5-12 Year Olds to Behave and Do as They're Told"* (the book is available in hard copy or audio at https://growingupchildren.com)

The recipe too that your own parents may have used to raise you, has now altered in that society has changed, and further, who said that the way that they raised you was the 'correct' way anyhow? Parenting is hard work. It can cause you to doubt yourself and can undermine your confidence. It can cause the marital relationship to suffer. Sole parenting too can be an exhausting process not to mention blended families and the like.

It's not surprising that parenting can trigger depression where parents start out with good intentions, but can feel overwhelmed, powerless, fatigued and generally at a loss.

Chapter 5 Summary

The causes of depression are not always immediately apparent, but generally fall into five main categories:

- Biology and genetics; it runs in families, and then there's the impact of brain chemicals and the structure of the brain

- History, upbringing, childhood and trauma; our past has a way of catching up with us

- Personality and temperament including negative thinking and a lack of coping skills and resilience

- External situations and circumstances, including the impact of things like work and finances

- Social relationships, including the loss of a loved one or the breakdown in social relationships and support networks as well as the demands of parenting

---

"If depression is creeping up and must be faced, learn something about the nature of the beast; you may escape without a mauling."

Dr R W Shepherd

CHAPTER 6

How is Depression Treated?

Introduction

The one aspect common to almost every form of depressive illness is that it must be treated. It cannot be taken lightly. People who are suffering from clinical depression cannot simply snap out of it and feel better spontaneously, and it won't just go away by itself.

With early diagnosis, intervention and competent care, however, most people can conquer clinical depression and resume normal social and occupational functioning.

Treatment approaches vary depending upon the nature and severity of the depression, but the prognosis is usually excellent, particularly when depressives actively participate in their own treatment. The most effective therapies are generally those which revolve around patient choice and participation. Patients who take responsibility for themselves, and who are motivated to improve, see positive outcomes and get better.

The more that depressed individuals do to help themselves, the greater the odds of long-term success. It really is a truism for all aspects of life, isn't it? The more you put in, the more you get out.

What are the goals of treatment for depression? In general, the immediate goals are to:

1. **Assess the danger to self and others**. Is the person suicidal? Is there danger of them hurting or injuring others, such as family members or work colleagues?

2. **Assess whether the person is a risk to the business**. For example, are they putting procedures, policies, or the business itself at risk by extraordinary behaviour, such as poor decision-making, especially in relation to spending money, or sexually promiscuous behaviour?

3. **Provide a safe environment**, both in the workplace and for the depressed individual. For example, if the depressive is aggressive or violent, involuntary commitment to a psychiatric institution for observation might be necessary.

4. **Determine the diagnosis, if possible**. Learn what treatment course may have been advised for them and if medications have been prescribed.

Once the immediate assessment goals are accomplished, further goals of therapy include:

1. Improve problem-solving and decision-making skills

2. Improve coping skills and the feeling of being in control

3. Develop and encourage use of a support system, such as family, friends, colleagues or management

4. Resolve any sense of loss (e.g., loss of a job, career, money or family)

5. Improve self-esteem and increase feelings of confidence

6. Restructure thought patterns and eliminate negative self-talk, faulty internal chatter and dialogue

7. Improve eating patterns and sleeping patterns, hygiene, and get into a regime of healthy living

8. Educate the depressive about the need to take medication, if applicable

6.1 Impact of Culture, Age, Gender and Race

To be effective, any treatment for depression must be tailored to an individual's circumstances, while reflecting sensitivity to the age, gender and racial and cultural characteristics that shape a person's self-image and identity. "Horses for courses", as they say.

6.1.1 Treating Different Cultures and Races

The "culturally competent" therapist, who understands the patient's group identity – history, traditions, beliefs, and value systems – has a better chance of engaging the patient, keeping them in treatment, and ultimately facilitating successful recovery. A lack of cultural competency can discourage minorities from seeking treatment because they believe treatment will be irrelevant, and that they will not be understood. Positive therapy experiences, on the other hand, can positively influence attitudes toward therapy and encourage others in the patient's community to seek help.[1]

Hence, as is often the case with other work situations, the manager needs to be sensitive to the culture of the individual. For example, some cultures have spiritual or mystical beliefs that could easily be misperceived as psychotic delusions by a culturally insensitive manager or therapist.

6.1.2 Treating Men Versus Treating Women

Since men and women often experience depression in vastly different ways, treatment must always be sensitive to the unique needs of the patient's gender.

For example, gender differences include:
- **Biological, physiological and anatomical differences**, such as female prenatal and postnatal hormonal influences, and male erectile dysfunction.
- **Socialisation**. For example, men are socialised to be tough and hide their feelings, whereas many women are socialised to believe they are the weaker sex.
- **Symptoms and danger signs**. For example, women are more prone to despair, helplessness and passivity, whereas men are more prone to expressing depression as anger, rage, or with reckless behaviour.

6.1.3 Treating Adolescents

As we all know, adolescents get depressed, and this often shows up at work. Clinical trials of adolescents with severe clinical depression have found that a combination of medication and psychotherapy is the most effective treatment option.[2]

6.1.4 Treating Seniors

The majority of older adults with depression improve when they receive treatment with an antidepressant, psychotherapy, or a combination of both. Research shows that medication alone and combination treatment are both effective in reducing the rate of depressive recurrences in older adults.

Psychotherapy alone can be effective, especially for seniors with minor depression, and for seniors who are unable or unwilling to take anti-depressant medication.

6.2 Pharmacological Treatments

Most doctors agree that anti-depressants are the first-line medications for treating clinical depression. In many cases, medication is the only treatment a depressive receives, since antidepressants are an inexpensive, fast-acting and convenient solution, and are readily available from general practitioners.

There is debate as to whether taking antidepressants really fixes the problem, but some people prefer a convenient quick fix, without having to get to the cause of their problem. Furthermore, not all drugs are considered equal. **Contrary to what the drug companies would have you believe, it has been argued that some anti-depressants are far more powerful than others in helping certain types of depression.**[3]

Furthermore, what isn't widely broadcast is that currently, doctors are speculating with their patients as to what drug might actually be most effective.

Dr Nick Martin from Brisbane's QIMR Berghofer Medical Research Institute is involved in an international study of genes and "regulatory switches" that might predispose some individuals towards depression.[4] He argues that finding the genes for depression will help determine why one person responds to a particular drug, but another doesn't. He goes on to say, that "the hope here is to try to get over that rather miserable cycle of prescribing failure which is hugely expensive and extremely stressful for the patient" and that we "will have a much higher success rate than if we just choose drugs at random which is pretty much what happens now".

Clearly, at this present time, **prescribing pharmaceuticals is not an exact science although doctors and the drug companies are unlikely to tell you that.**

Nevertheless, most treatment guidelines or protocols indicate that anti-depressants may take many weeks to work. However, actual clinical experience suggests that there ought to be some improvement within the first ten days or so whether that be in general mood, sleep or other features. With melancholic and psychotic depression, however, results can take longer. For most clients, if there are no signs of improvement within **the first two weeks**, either the dosage of the anti-depressant ought to be increased or another class of anti-depressant ought to be trialled.

It is also important to understand that there is no universal method of labelling drugs so anti-depressants can be classified according to what is called "generation" or the "chemical characteristics" of the drug or the "function" of the drug. To expand on this, **"generation"** refers to the period of discovery of the drug and its release onto the market. For example, first-generation anti-depressants appeared in the late 1950s and were trialled in the 1960s. Second-generation anti-depressants emerged in the 1970s and early 1980s, and third-generation drugs have been available since the 1990s.[5]

In relation to the "**chemical characteristics**", of the drug classes, this is determined by their nuclear structure. "Tricyclic" drugs have a three-ring structure, tetracyclic four, and recently developed "bicyclic" drugs have a two-ring structure.

In regards to "**function**" of the drug, it is true that most anti-depressants have multiple actions, however, many work by inhibiting the reuptake or re-absorption of one or more different neurotransmitters (including serotonin, noradrenaline and dopamine) at the nerve synapses, therefore increasing the concentration of the neurotransmitter. While first-generation anti-depressants (the tricyclics and MAOIs) act on multiple neurotransmitters, the newer drugs are more selective in the neurotransmitters that they target. This selectivity is reflected in the drug class name that is allocated, such as selective serotonin reuptake inhibitor (SSRI) or selective noradrenaline reuptake inhibitor (SNRI).

What are the most commonly used drugs to treat depression? See Appendix C for a table showing the range of anti-depressants that are currently available and Appendix D for the range of side effects.

1. Tricyclics or tricyclic antidepressants (TCAs)

From the 1960s through the 1980s, tricyclics were the first line of treatment for severe clinical depression. They include amitriptyline, clomipramine, desipramine, doxepin, imipramine, and nortriptyline. Most of these medications affect two chemical neurotransmitters, namely norepinephrine and serotonin. Although the tricyclics have been shown to be as effective in treating depression as the newer antidepressants, their side effects usually are more unpleasant.[6] For that reason, tricyclics generally are used today as a second- or third-line treatment.

These older tricyclic drugs (TCAs) and irreversible monoamine oxidase inhibitors (MAOIs) appear to be more effective than selective serotonin reuptake inhibitors (SSRIs) for both melancholic and psychotic depression.[2] Research conducted showed that for patients with melancholic depression who are over 60 years of age, the chance of responding to a TCA was four times as great as for an SSRI.

The more common side-effects caused by these TCA medications include the following:[6]
- Drowsiness, fatigue and tiredness
- Dry mouth
- Constipation
- Dizziness
- Weight gain
- Rapid heart rate or irregular heart rhythm
- Difficulty passing urine
- Blurring of vision

2. Monoamine oxidase inhibitors (MAOIs)

These include isocarboxazid, phenelzine and tranylcypromine. Researchers believe that the MAOIs relieve depression by preventing the enzyme monoamine oxidase from metabolizing the neurotransmitters norepinephrine, noradrenaline, serotonin and dopamine. Also used extensively from the 1960s through the 1980s, MAOIs are effective for some people with clinical depression who do not respond to the other anti-depressants, and are also effective for treating panic disorder and bipolar depression. MAOIs are used less commonly than the other antidepressants because they can have serious side effects, and because patients need to avoid certain medications and foods that contain high levels of tyramine while taking MAOIs.

3. Selective serotonin reuptake inhibitors (SSRIs)

These are the newest and most widely prescribed group of anti-depressants which revolutionized the field of psychopharmacology.[7] They drugs include citalopram, escitalopram, fluvoxamine, fluoxetine, paroxetine, and sertraline. Current practice suggests that approximately 60-70% of clinical depressives who are treated with SSRIs will experience complete relief.[3,8]

For non-melancholic depression, the SSRIs and dual action drugs (i.e. serotonin and noradrenaline reuptake inhibitors – SNRIs) are the benchmark anti-depressants.[3]

Popular brands of SSRIs, such as Prozac, Zoloft and Paxil, appear to relieve symptoms of depression by blocking the re-absorption of serotonin by certain nerve cells in the brain. This leaves more serotonin available, which enhances neurotransmission, and in the process boosts confidence and self-esteem, restores a balanced and more optimistic perspective on life, and helps promote an inner resilience that better enables the depressive to cope with stress. When the immediate reuptake of serotonin is prevented, more of these precious brain chemicals remain available to do their intended work.

These medications have been shown to have fewer side-effects than other antidepressants, with similar cost effectiveness. Typically, SSRIs take four to eight weeks to reach maximal therapeutic effect. For depressives with severe, recurrent symptoms, long-term maintenance dosages may be required to prevent relapses. The side effects, however, of selective serotonin reuptake inhibitors may include:

- Nausea and feeling sick
- Feeling agitated, shaky or anxious
- Insomnia
- Headaches
- Indigestion and stomach aches
- Dizziness
- Diarrhoea or constipation
- Loss of appetite
- Insomnia
- Erectile difficulties or delayed orgasm

4. Serotonin and norepinephrine reuptake inhibitors (SNRIs)

These include venlafaxine and duloxetine. Venlafaxine in particular, has performed well compared with other anti-depressants in terms of efficacy and cost effectiveness, and it has minimal side-effects. SNRIs are generally second-line, and not as well tolerated as SSRIs.

Common side effects caused by these medications include:

- Nausea and loss of appetite
- Anxiety and nervousness
- Headache
- Insomnia
- Tiredness

The pharmacological treatment of bipolar disorder, however, is more complicated. Mood stabilizers such as lithium are generally prescribed. For manic phases of bipolar disorder, mood stabilisers are often combined with antipsychotics, which both relieve psychotic symptoms and control behaviour. The depressive phases of bipolar disorder are often treated with a combination of mood stabilisers and anti-depressants.

6.3 Psychosocial Therapies

There are a number of therapies available in the marketplace, but which ones really work? Which are the most highly regarded?

Before we look at individual therapies or treatments, let's ask a more basic question: How does psychotherapy help people recover from depression? According to the American Psychological Association,[1] psychotherapy sessions can help people in the following ways:

- **Pinpointing the life problems that contribute to their depression** and helping them understand which aspects of those problems they may be able to solve or improve upon. A trained therapist (e.g., a psychologist, psychiatrist or social worker) can help depressed patients **identify options and set**

realistic goals that improve the client's mental and emotional well-being. Therapists also help individuals **identify how they have successfully dealt with similar feelings** if they have been depressed in the past. (*What has worked in the past and can we use this again?*)

- **Identifying negative or distorted thinking patterns** that contribute to feelings of hopelessness and helplessness. For example, depressed individuals may tend to over-generalise, that is, to think of circumstances in terms of "always" or "never". They may also take events personally all or most of the time. (*What are they saying to themselves to catastrophise a situation or event?*)

- **Exploring other learned thoughts and behaviours that create problems and contribute to depression.** For example, therapists can help depressed individuals understand and improve patterns of interacting with other people that contribute to their depression. (*What are they doing or not doing which means that they are not relating to or connecting well with others?*)

- **Helping people regain a sense of control and pleasure in life.** Psychotherapy helps people see their choices in life, as well as gradually incorporate enjoyable, fulfilling activities back into their lives. (*What do they like to do that gives them pleasure and enjoyment? Have they stopped doing certain things that previously gave them some pleasure?*)

Let's look at these various treatments in more detail.

6.3.1 Cognitive-Behavioural Therapy (CBT)

Without doubt, this is the treatment of choice.[9,10,11] It's the most popular therapy when it comes to depression. Cognitive-behavioural therapy (or cognitive-behaviour therapy, CBT) focuses primarily on the connection between thoughts, feelings and behaviour.

It is based on the principle that destructive or inappropriate behaviours can only be corrected by altering the thought processes behind those behaviours. That is, you act out being angry or aggressive because you feel angry due to your angry thoughts about a situation. Likewise, you feel happy because you think happy thoughts.

In simple terms, the client needs to change the thoughts that bring about angry feelings, which in turn cause them to get angry and act in a particular way. It's about changing faulty thinking and creating a new mind set.[11]

"Man is disturbed not by events, but by the view he takes of them."

Epictetus,
Greek philosopher

Figure 6.1 on the next page shows the connection between a situation that occurs and the behaviour that might result, based on the thoughts that immediately eventuate, followed by the feelings that occur, leading to a particular action or behaviour. Of course, this all occurs in the wink of an eye, as it were.

FIGURE 6.1

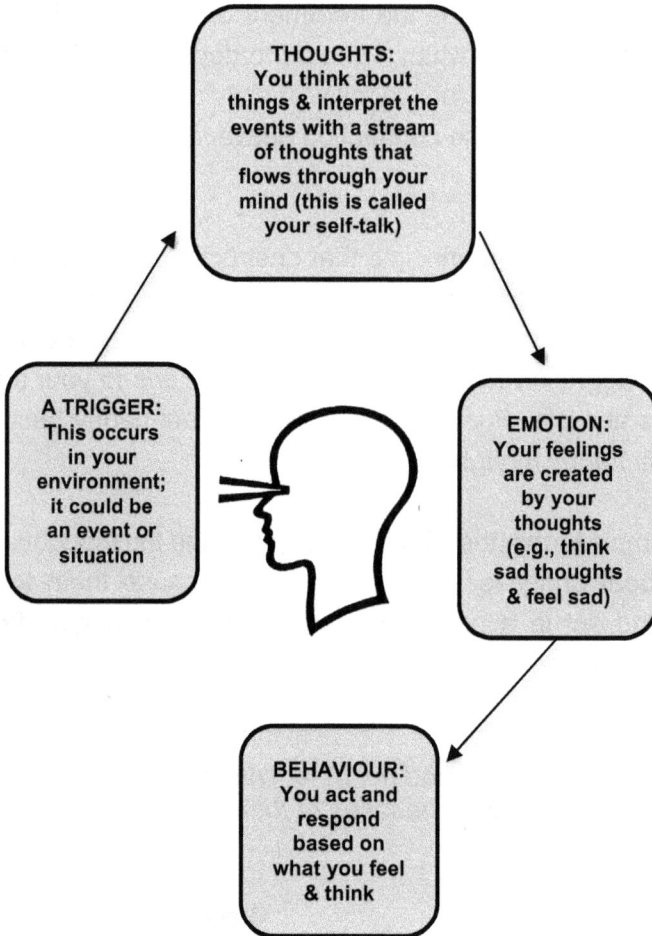

THOUGHTS:
You think about things & interpret the events with a stream of thoughts that flows through your mind (this is called your self-talk)

A TRIGGER:
This occurs in your environment; it could be an event or situation

EMOTION:
Your feelings are created by your thoughts (e.g., think sad thoughts & feel sad)

BEHAVIOUR:
You act and respond based on what you feel & think

All experiences are processed through your brain and given conscious meaning before you experience an emotional response and behave accordingly.

CBT focuses on helping clients recognise the thought patterns that provoke self-damaging behaviours – their beliefs, attitudes, and mental imagery or pictures. Once an individual can recognise perceptions which are distorted, or which fuel negative thinking, it's easier to break bad habits and stop reacting in destructive ways or in ways that self-sabotage.

"You largely constructed your depression. It wasn't given to you. Therefore, you can deconstruct it."

Albert Ellis, 1913-2007
American psychologist

The goal of CBT is to get patients to actively participate in getting better. In CBT, the therapist-patient relationship is more collaborative than it was in turn-of-the-century treatment models in which the therapist merely offered analysis and insight. CBT offers faster results and lower recurrence rates.

CBT is one of the most effective and widely used treatments for clinical depression. For mild to moderate depression, CBT can be as effective as anti-depressant medication, and can help prevent further episodes of depression. Recent research suggests that CBT, paired with appropriate anti-depressant medication, is also often the most effective course for treating moderate to severe depression.

CBT can also be highly effective for treating thought disorders such as schizophrenia, as well as the thought disorder component of clinical depression, or any disorder in which thought disruption is caused by distortions in judgment.

"For as long as I can remember, I've suffered from anxiety and low self-esteem. I know that I'm a negative or pessimistic thinker. My family calls me a worry-wart. My local doctor insisted that he refer me to a psychologist who specialised in cognitive-behavioural therapy. I really didn't want to go, but decided in the end that I would. CBT challenged the way that I saw things and challenged my habitual negative way of thinking, and I became more realistic in my perceptions. I was able, for example, to see things that I would have once seen as negative or awful in a more positive light.

I saw the psychologist for about four months and occasionally go back for a 'refresher'. But I can honestly say that it changed my 'head space' and certainly changed my life around.

Looking back, I think that my constant anxiety made me depressed.

I still remember, though, the quote that I learned: 'It's not what happens to you that's important, it's your interpretation of what happens to you that's important.' It's true you know."

Examples of depressive thought disorders which are negative or faulty in some way might include:

1. **Filtering:** You magnify the negative details of a situation, while filtering out all the positive aspects – looking at the threats in a situation instead of looking for a challenge or an opportunity (e.g., *"I've lost my job – I'm ruined – it's the end"*).

2. **Polarised thinking:** Things are either black or white, good or bad. You have to be perfect or you're a failure. There is no middle ground (e.g., *"Coming in second is not good enough"*, or *"Why didn't you get an 'A' grade instead of a 'B+' grade?"*).

3. **Catastrophising:** You expect disaster. You notice or hear about a problem and make mountains out of molehills; stress is exaggerated (e.g., saying words like *"terrible" and "awful"*, and phrases like, *"I can't stand it"*, and *"It's the end of the world"*).

4. **Personalisation:** Thinking that everything people do or say is some kind of reaction to you. You compare yourself to others, trying to determine who is smarter, better looking, etc. (e.g., *"She's better than me"*, *"He's got all the looks and talent"*, *"Why are they looking at me all the time?"* or *"What's wrong with me?"*).

5. **Blaming others:** You hold other people responsible for your pain or for your situation when things have not gone as you would have wished (e.g., *"It's all management's fault"*, *"My rotten team made me fail"*, or *"They made me do it"*).

6. **Living negatively in the past:** Going back over spilled milk or re-analysing the past (e.g., *" If only..."* *"If only I'd taken that promotion"*, *"If only I hadn't joined that team"*, or *"If only I'd taken more time over it"*).

A typical CBT treatment course consists of 12 to 20 one-hour therapy sessions. The therapist notes the negative or faulty thinking and shows the client how to challenge these distortions and turn them around, thereby altering the processing of information that has been creating and perpetuating the depressed mood.

Cognitive-behavioural therapy helps clients change the negative expectations, assumptions and beliefs that are damaging their self-images, their relationships, and their lives.

6.3.2 Interpersonal Psychotherapy (IPT)

Life is also about relationships or connections. Whether we like it or not, we're connected! "No man is an island", as the saying goes.

Interpersonal psychotherapy (IPT) treats clinical depression by focusing on interpersonal relationships and their contributions to mood abnormalities.[3,12] The goal of IPT is to help the depressive evaluate and improve interpersonal skills – how they relate to others – including family, friends and colleagues.

Even if the depression is not caused by interpersonal events, it almost invariably ends up with an interpersonal component to it. The relationships of the depressed individual are impacted whether that be in the family, socially or at work.

Work colleagues, for example, notice that the person is somehow different ("He's not like he used to be", "She's changed", or "He's more moody and grumpy these days"). They tend to stay away or not talk to the person as much, and instead confide in other work peers or gossip about what they have seen, noticed or heard.

IPT often focuses on those events that are critical to the onset and/or long-term maintenance of depression, including the following:

1. **Interpersonal disputes,** in which the person is no longer talking to a family member because of a falling-out. This may extend to the wider family of in-laws and other extended family groups, who may take sides.

2. **Conflicts** in which co-workers have a disagreement which has been a kind of running battle over months or even years.

3. **Role transitions**. For example, the person has been asked to care for an elderly parent when none of the other siblings want to take responsibility. Another example is when an individual has had to take over a job role that doesn't really suit them, and they have been given little, if any, training. A person sees no way out because of financial commitments, such as a mortgage.

4. **Complex bereavements** that extend beyond the normal bereavement period, in which the person somehow feels responsible for the death.

Many psychotherapists believe that IPT can be as effective as anti-depressant medication for short-term treatment of depression. IPT also works well in conjunction with medications. Like cognitive-behavioural therapy, IPT typically follows a treatment course of 12 to 20 sessions.

6.3.3 Social Treatments and Psycho-education

None of us live in a vacuum. There is a context in which we all live. Social treatments address the context of depression, including social stressors that may be provoking a depressed mood. People are less happy when they don't feel productive or they are financially distressed, so effective resources might include community support groups, vocational rehabilitation, job placement assistance, and assistance in securing affordable housing or disability income.

Psycho-education can be a valuable social intervention. The family, friends and colleagues who comprise the depressive's social support network often need to be educated about the symptoms, course and treatment of depression. Typically, the family and friends are keen to help out, but don't quite know how. The treating professional, whether that be a psychologist, psychiatrist, etc., can direct these efforts.

Education can also go a long way toward mitigating the stigma attached to mental illness and improving the patient's ability to adhere to treatment and avoid relapses.

6.4 Institutionalisation

Institutionalisation is one of the last resort treatments, generally reserved for situations in which emergency intervention is required, or the patient is a danger to themselves and/or others.

For example, if a patient is threatening to end their life (and may already have tried), this may be sufficient reason to take them to the Emergency Department of the local hospital or perhaps place them in a psychiatric hospital where they can be monitored twenty-four hours a day.

If a patient is so depressed that they are acting out by damaging property and/or threatening people, then it will be important to call the police and it may be most appropriate for the individual to be institutionalised for a period.

Institutionalisation, though, is expensive, invasive, time consuming, and can, for some patients, exacerbate symptoms.

6.5 Electroconvulsive Therapy (ECT)

There is a treatment of last resort; very last resort. It's called electroconvulsive therapy (ECT), commonly known as "electro-shock therapy". If you have seen the movie, *One Flew Over the Cuckoo's Nest*, starring Jack Nicholson, then you saw the Hollywood version of ECT. Some would suggest that the real thing is very much the same as the movie version.

This treatment is typically reserved for severely suicidal patients and the most treatment-resistant cases. ECT has always been stigma-loaded, and is complex to administer. ECT occurs under general anaesthesia. An electric stimulus is administered to the patient, causing a brain seizure that is thought to have an enhancing effect on neurotransmitters such as dopamine and serotonin.

The course for ECT is generally six to eight treatments, three treatments per week. After this course of treatment, mood symptoms vanish in as many as 85% of patients. ECT can be a first-line treatment for patients who have successfully responded to ECT in the past, as well as for patients who have a life-threatening illness that requires immediate treatment (e.g., severe physical exhaustion or dehydration that occurs when a patient won't or can't sleep or take fluids or food), or who are pregnant and do not want to expose the developing foetus to medication.

According to sources such as the Mayo Clinic,[13] ECT can have severe side effects, including:

- Short-term memory loss; it can also affect long-term memory and the formation of new memories, though memory loss is usually temporary
- Physical side effects; nausea, headache, jaw pain or muscle aches
- Confusion; not knowing where you are or why you're where you are
- Medical complications; heart problems

6.6 Extensions to Therapy

6.6.1 Exercise

There is a relationship between exercise and mood. It comes as no surprise to learn that inactive people generally have a lower mood than do active people. Hence, most therapists agree that physical exercise ought to be a part of any depression therapy. Depression makes your body heavy and sluggish, and being heavy and sluggish exacerbates depression – another vicious cycle.

Energetic, aerobic exercise is an outlet for releasing negative emotions, as well as a neurotransmitter stimulant. Exercise produces endorphins, which are effectively endogenous, or a kind of natural morphine that energises the body and mind and endows a sense of well-being. Physical fitness also boosts self-image and confidence.

"Exercise Found Effective Against Depression" was the news headline that announced the findings of a major study into the relationship between exercise and depression.[13] The article went on to say that, "A brisk 30-minute walk or jog three times a week may be just as effective in relieving major depression as are standard antidepressant drugs". The study related to this article was conducted at Duke University Medical Center in North Carolina and published in 1999. A sample of 156 volunteers with clinical depression were randomly placed into one of three treatment groups:

Group 1: Medicated using sertraline, which has the trade name of Zoloft

Group 2: 30 minute exercise, 3 times per week

Group 3: Zoloft plus the exercise

The volunteers were assessed again after 16 weeks. What were the results for each of these three groups?

Table 6.1

	Zoloft	Exercise	Combination
Improvement after 4 months	66%	60%	69%

Improvement in patients exposed to medication alone, exercise alone, and a combination of both medication and exercise.

The results are fascinating in that the researchers point out that the variance between these three groups is not statistically different. Since the improvement rate was statistically the same for those who only took Zoloft and those who only exercised, the researchers offered the opinion that exercise may be more beneficial than the drug itself, because patients who exercised were actually taking more of an active role in trying to get better, which could lead to other benefits not realised.

Nevertheless, the results speak for themselves. Don't overlook exercise as an important adjunct to therapy.

"If I had not already been meditating, I would certainly have had to start. I've treated my own depression for many years with exercise and meditation, and I've found that to be a tremendous help."

Judy Collins, 1939-
American folk singer and songwriter

6.6.2 Nutrition

You've heard the saying, "You are what you eat". Many believe that illness can be treated by providing the body and brain with the correct amounts of nutrients.

Evidence suggests that diet can play a huge role in mood, energy and a sense of well-being. For example, high-fibre foods boost energy and metabolism; the omega-3 fatty acids found in fish may help bolster mood. Some research suggests that high intake of caffeine, sugar and alcohol can contribute to depressed mood.

John was a district Director in the Education Department and was referred to me by his doctor because he was depressed and generally not coping. John reported that he was certainly struggling, and felt overwhelmed, as well as being fatigued and constantly tired.

When asked about his daily habits, including food and drink, John said that he would get up in the morning ("I drag myself out of bed"), would not eat any breakfast ("No time for breakfast"), and survive through the day on about 32 cups of coffee!

Further, he said that when he got home at night, he would have a big meal, and then generally wash it down with a bottle of red.

Little wonder that he was so fatigued and was starting to have tremors in his hands, as well as being almost burnt-out.

Note this news story released by the BBC in England on January 16, 2006:

BBC News Report: One man speaks about how he feels cutting out certain foods made a world of difference to his life.

Brian Godfrey suffered from chronic depression for about 40 years. He first started having trouble when he was a teenager and over the years tried everything from drugs to psychotherapy.

By the 1960s the situation had got so bad that he was thinking about suicide. "It was terrible, I would wake up in the morning with a fuzzy head and just could not get going. I felt tired and depressed. Some days it would be so bad I would lay in bed crying."

Mr. Godfrey said it was only when it became clear the advice doctors were giving him was not going to work that he decided to look for something else, "I went to the library and found a book about food intolerance".

The 71-year-old then cut out wheat and dairy and within three weeks was feeling better. "It was a miracle. I just woke up one morning and my problems had gone."

In time, Mr. Godfrey, from London, also stopped eating grains, eggs, chocolate, coffee, tea and his favourite drink, Guinness. "I used to love to have a drink of Guinness after a meal, but that had to go. It was hard."

"I am very careful what I eat now, especially when I go out for a meal. My main diet is meat, fish, vegetables and fruit and I only eat organic food."

And Mr. Godfrey, who is now completely free of the severe depression which plagued him during the first half of his life, said other people should consider altering their diets if they are having problems.

"It is becoming clear food is linked to mental illness. I would say that the things you most like are what most cause you harm. It is worth trying to cut them out", he says.

So what are some tips for eating sensibly to alleviate depression?

1. Eat by the clock, not by your stomach.

2. Make it nutritious.

3. Make it easy to prepare.

4. Avoid fast food outlets and processed food.

5. Avoid refined sugar and foods which cause a sharp rise in blood sugar.

6. Stay with whole grains and brown rice.

7. Give up soft drinks (which have about 10 teaspoons of sugar in every can).

6.7 Alternative Therapies

Alternative treatments are abounding. They are becoming more and more popular for a range of ailments, and practitioners are experimenting with alternative therapies for treating depression. Here are some of the popular therapies:

- **Acupuncture** may help balance blood flow throughout the body and resolve underlying energy imbalances contributing to depression. Stimulating acupuncture points has been shown to release endorphins and enkephalins, evoking a calming, mood-elevating effect.

- **Acupressure** can alleviate physical symptoms as well as the lethargy of mild depression. Acupressure is performed by applying steady, firm pressure on specific points along the body. According to Chinese medicine, depression can occur when you repress certain emotions, such as anger or guilt.

- **Biofeedback (Neurotherapy):** Evidence suggests that receiving EEG (brainwave) feedback can reduce the severity of depression. Biofeedback is obtained by connecting the subject to an apparatus that measures physiological responses, such as heart rate, muscle tension, skin temperature and brain waves, while the subject focuses on a sensory cue to help them relax. The goal of biofeedback is to alter brainwave patterns through training. Biofeedback training is a systematised approach to learning relaxation and more positive physiological responses. Refocusing energy in a self-empowering way enables the subject to have greater control over their autonomic nervous system reactions (heart rate, blood pressure), including those triggered by stress.[15]

- **Transcranial magnetic stimulation (TMS):** Some National Institute of Mental Health (NIMH) studies in the U.S. have shown that repetitive magnetic stimulation of the brain's left prefrontal cortex may help some depressed patients in a way similar to electroconvulsive therapy (ECT), but without ECT's side effects.

- **Meditation** can be useful in relieving mild depression.[16] Meditation's calming effect helps ease tension, improve concentration, increase awareness of feelings, and relieve negative thoughts.

- **Hypnotherapy** can be effective in treating mild depression and anxiety, particularly as a relaxation technique. Clinical hypnotherapy can help bring repressed memories to the surface in order to deal with them.

- **Herbal and homeopathic remedies,** such as St. John's Wort, Ignatia, Pulsatilla, Sepia, and Aurum have been suggested to help alleviate the blues. With St. John's Wort in particular, data suggests that it is an effective anti-depressant and comparable to the tricyclic anti-depressants.[3,17] However, it also seems that it is likely to be of most assistance to those who are experiencing non-melancholic depression rather than the more severe depressions.

- **Aromatherapy:** Some researchers[18] believe that mild depression can be mitigated by applying certain essential oils on the skin: basil, bergamot, cedarwood, clary sage, frankincense, geranium, grapefruit, lavender, lemon, jasmine, myrrh, neroli, rose, sandalwood, spruce, orange, or ylang ylang.

Chapter 6 Summary

There are treatments for depression, and they work. Of course, it does behove the treating professional to get the diagnosis right (non-melancholic depression, melancholic depression, psychotic depression or bipolar depression), and then to apply the most appropriate treatment.

On top of the list are anti-depressants and/or psychotherapy in various forms. The most popular therapy is cognitive-behavioural therapy (CBT), which focuses on changing the negative thinking and faulty thought patterns which trigger a depressed mood.

Other therapies include interpersonal therapy (IPT), social treatments and psycho-education. A very last resort is electroconvulsive therapy (ECT). Finally, there are the range of alternative therapies.

"Good humour is a tonic for mind and body. It is the best antidote for anxiety and depression. It is a business asset. It attracts and keeps friends. It lightens human burdens. It is the direct route to serenity and contentment."

Grenville Kleiser, 1868-1935
American author

CHAPTER 7

Recognising Depression in the Workplace

Introduction

Nigel was a 44-year-old teacher who presented to me saying
that he didn't think teaching was the career for him any longer.
He looked despondent and he spoke slowly. He said that
when he was going through university, he was quite excited
about the prospect of teaching as a profession, and about
being able to make a difference in young people's lives.

But over the years, all this had changed. Behavioural problems
in the classroom had escalated, and he was asked to "main
stream" more children with disabilities of some kind. He also
believed he was being asked to do more with less. The
paperwork, for example, had increased exponentially, and he
felt that he had less time to devote to real teaching. He said it
was more about catering to the Education Department Central
Office with their demands of reporting than it was about
teaching children. He also said that parents had now become

more assertive and at times aggressive re expectations and wants for their child.

He said that his colleagues would sometimes talk to him in the staff room about the fact that he seemed withdrawn and "not himself". He said that the school principal asked to see him and commented that she had noticed that he didn't turn up to as many meetings, and no longer attended social gatherings or get-togethers. She also indicated that he was absent more days than in previous years. She said the curriculum coordinator had mentioned to her that Nigel no longer volunteered for any curriculum tasks and that he had missed some deadlines, which was seen as quite uncharacteristic.

Nigel said that the principal showed concern and wanted to know how he was doing and if anything was wrong.

7.1 What Should You Be On The Lookout For?

Who's depressed...the man who eats too little, or the man who eats too much? The woman who can't sleep, or the woman who can't stay awake? The perennially sad employee who rarely seems to react to what others say and do, or the agitated, flighty employee who overreacts to everything? The man who seemed fine until his mid-30s, or the man who has exhibited occasional symptoms of depression since childhood?

As diverse as these profiles may seem, each of these people shows signs of depression. It's easy to think of depression as one thing. It's not.

Depression interferes with work in many ways, and problematic behaviour increases as symptoms escalate. The **three key indicators** that a worker might be struggling with their mental health includes the following:

1. Decline in productivity
2. Increased absenteeism
3. Changes in moods

More specifically, **the more common signs** of work depression include:

- Withdrawal or isolation from other people
- Procrastination, missed deadlines, reduced productivity, subpar performance in tasks, increased errors, or difficulty making decisions
- Late arrival at work, missed meetings or absent days
- Seeming indifference, forgetfulness, detachment, and disinterest in things
- An appearance of tiredness for most or part of the day (and maybe taking afternoon naps at work or during work hours)
- Irritability, anger, feeling overwhelmed, or getting very emotional during conversations
- Poor self-hygiene or significant change in appearance
- Lack of confidence while attempting tasks

Human behavioural analysis is not a precise science. Differentiating a depressive disorder from a low mood or personality characteristic often requires sorting many factors in the individual's life, including a personal history that you, as a manager or human resources professional, may not be aware.

It is not your job, however, to make a diagnosis. Your job as the boss is to simply observe, and then, if possible, to refer your employee to a mental health professional.

A tip that many general practitioners use is called the "**Rule of Five**".[1] If a patient presents with **five or more symptoms or physical complaints**, the possibility of them having an underlying mental disorder, including depression, is highly likely.

It is recognised that at least 69% of patients with severe clinical depression present to their general practitioner with somatic complaints such as backache, headaches, sleeplessness, eating problems, bowel problems, high blood pressure, and so on.

At work, staff often talk about their ailments and aches and pains. It's not a golden rule, but if you notice that someone seems down, and they also have a number of physical or somatic complaints (i.e. the Rule of Five), then you ought to be alerted to a possible depressive disorder.

Research by the National Business Group on Health in the U.S. showed that clinical depression is the *most frequent* diagnosis associated with **absence from the workplace**. It is also responsible for more missed days at work (709 per 1,000 employees) than arthritis (504), hypertension (484), asthma (438), or substance abuse (166).[2] Does depression cut profits and productivity? You bet it does.

Prior to determining whether intervention is required for an employee you suspect is depressed, you should assess the extent of the employee's impairment as quickly as possible. The longer depression goes untreated, the more difficult it is to treat, and the more widespread – and potentially devastating – its impact on the workplace.

7.1.1 Two Common Assessment Mistakes

A decline in an individual's performance does not automatically indicate clinical depression. It's easy to make these mistakes when assessing depression:

1. Focusing on the person's anxiety, alcoholism, or psychotic symptoms and ignoring underlying symptoms of depression or dysthymia. *Always look for a mood disorder first, even if the chief complaint is something else.*

2. Diagnosing depression and failing to notice the presence of alcoholism or another disorder, such as an anxiety disorder or personality disorder. *Never assume that a mood disorder is the person's only disorder.*

Assessment can be complicated by the fact that a depressive may complain of physical symptoms, such as backaches or insomnia, not realising, or perhaps not acknowledging, that the root cause of the physical problem is depression.

Evaluating depressive symptoms is especially difficult in individuals who are suffering from a general medical condition such as cancer, diabetes, stroke or heart disease. Could the person's symptoms be produced by drugs or a non-psychiatric medical illness? Some of the symptoms of a major depressive episode are identical to the symptoms of general medical conditions, for example, weight loss with untreated diabetes, or fatigue with cancer.

Bob was the general manager of a commercial fit-out company with a turnover of $20 million per year. His company would start with the bare bones of a building's interior and then design and create the internal work-space with floor coverings, painting, offices, corridors, workstations, communication, computer hubs and the like.

He rang to say that he was concerned about one of the managers of his fit-out teams. He had had a number of chats with him at his office and at the coffee shop across the road. Bob was concerned about a range of things, including the manager's deteriorating communication with his team, a lack of leadership, missing deadlines, and a general lethargic attitude and approach.

Following their conversation, the manager indicated that he thought he may be depressed. Bob said that this was really out of his field and he really didn't know what to do ("I'm way out of my depth on this one"), so he thought he'd better ring me for advice. He said that he had told the manager that he would be ringing me and that he would get back with him immediately with a plan to go forward.

7.2 Deciding to Step In: Should You Intervene?

Many employers want to respond compassionately to employee health problems, but managers walk a fine line with employees. When is personal *too* personal? How strongly should an employer urge an employee to seek treatment?

In workplace depression management, knowing when to intervene is the first hurdle to leap. Historically, employers have been hesitant to take an active role in encouraging treatment. However, skyrocketing medical costs and anti-discrimination laws have provided employers with the incentive to take a more proactive approach to providing good mental health care for their employees.

Many organisations have found that teaming up with Employee Assistance Programs (EAPs) makes for an effective partnership in the battle against workplace depression.

These programs are out-sourced to specialist groups of psychologists for example, where confidential counselling is provided and paid for by the company. EAPs are programs which operate within an organisation to identify troubled employees, motivate those employees to resolve their troubles, and provide access to counselling or treatment for those who need it.

How do you know when to intervene? The following two litmus tests are a good place to start:

1. **When the employee becomes a management problem or there is an obvious performance problem.** For example, for a few weeks you've observed several of the red flags itemized in 7.1 above or 7.2.1 below.

2. **When you have reason to believe the employee may be at risk for suicide.** The suicide risk assessment in 7.2.2 below can help you assess risk.

7.2.1 Red Flags

If an employee is depressed, you'll begin to spot the red flags as hinted at in 7.1 above. Symptoms common to depressed workers typically include:

- Decreased energy and productivity, yet working – or trying to work
- Inability to concentrate, forgetfulness, distraction
- Inability to organise or delegate tasks
- Making mistakes more frequently
- Morale problems, which might include lack of cooperation and disputes with colleagues
- Safety risks, accidents
- Absenteeism and being late for work or meetings
- Frequent statements about being tired all the time
- Complaints about unexplained aches and pains
- A decline in personal hygiene
- Alcohol or drug abuse

Depressives are usually not great dressers. Many find that bathing uses up too much energy. Many have difficulty staying alert during meetings and completing tasks well and on time.

Depressed people often work too hard and get nowhere. One of the most common strategies for avoiding emotions is "busy-ness". They never seem to make as much progress as their activity level warrants. There is a frantic, driven, compulsive flavour to their methods; this is particularly true of agitated depressives. The irony is that they will only recover if they change their habits, but since they're proud of their hard work and stamina, they can't bear to question that aspect of themselves.

7.2.2 Suicide Risk Assessment

The assessment of depression always requires an assessment of the risk of suicide. And risk of suicide, of course, is perhaps the very best reason to intervene.

Suicide risk is especially high for depressed individuals who have:

- Exhibited psychotic behaviours (i.e. losing contact with reality)
- A history of previous suicide attempts
- A family history of completed suicides
- A substance abuse problem
- Experienced recent bereavement

A preliminary interview with a depressed employee may help indicate whether the employee is at risk for suicide, particularly when the interviewing manager or HR professional has an established, comfortable relationship with the depressed employee.

Suicide risk assessment generally involves a graduated approach to asking questions – from the least threatening to the most threatening. A typical approach used by psychotherapists that can be used by a supportive manager or HR professional might be as follows: [3]

1. Begin with broad, unthreatening remarks, such as: *"Things seem to have been pretty bad for you recently. Do you sometimes feel overwhelmed or perhaps hopeless?"*

2. Next, ask questions that probe whether the individual has passive thoughts about dying: *"Do you sometimes not want to wake up in the morning?"* or

perhaps, *"Does it seem like life isn't worth living?"*

3. Then, ask questions that specifically target suicidal thoughts and intentions: *"Have you thought of harming yourself?"*

4. Finally, try to determine whether the person is formulating a specific plan, often referred to as *suicide ideation: "What have you considered doing? How far have you gone with this? What has stopped you?"*

7.3 Depression Screenings

A 2004 University of Michigan survey revealed that more than three-quarters of managers believe that the cost of lost productivity due to depression is greater than the cost of treating depression, yet only 11% facilitate employee screenings.[4]

This is **not** to suggest that managers now have to be mental health experts and be able to diagnose! As managers, you already have too much to do and not enough hours in the day to do it. Some HR managers, directors or consultants, though, may wish to undertake some initial screening in order to be confident of a referral to a mental health professional. Such screening programs can be a compulsory part of a wellness check-up, along with fitness screening, and can be conducted in privacy.

Numerous screening measures have been specifically designed to detect depression. However, it also needs to be clearly said that managers and HR professionals may not need to use in-depth diagnostic tools if they can simply **ask two questions** of the employee or staff member, namely:

1. *"Over the past two weeks, have you ever felt down, depressed, or hopeless?"*

2. *"Have you felt little interest or pleasure in doing things?"*

Selection of a screening measure, whether it be the two simple questions listed above or a more thorough diagnostic tool, is the first and most important step in the process of managing depression. Depression screenings, which are a common diagnostic tool used by doctors, psychologists and EAPs, can be an effective early detection tool. The tests are easy to administer and require only a few minutes to take. The HR manager or the employee assistance provider are generally in the best position to administer one of the methods listed below.

Commonly used depression screening tests include:

- **Beck Depression Inventory (BDI-II)**
  This test is a widely-used, self-rating inventory that consists of 21 questions, each of which describes depression behaviours (e.g., sleeplessness, feelings of sadness, loss of energy). The total score (maximum 63) measures the depth of depression. It takes about 5-10 minutes to complete.[5,6]

- **Center for Epidemiological Studies Depression (CES-D)**
  This 20-item test is a self-report measure designed for use in the general population. It takes about 5-10 minutes to complete. Scoring CES-D is completed by totalling the numbers next to each response.[7]

- **Zung Depression Rating Scale**
  This is a 20-item rating scale. Scoring of the Zung scale is slightly more difficult because the raw score must be converted using a table. This test takes about 5-10 minutes to complete.[8]

"Mental pain is less dramatic than physical pain, but it is more common and also more hard to bear. The frequent attempt to conceal mental pain increases the burden: it is easier to say, 'My tooth is aching' than to say, 'My heart is broken' "

C.S. Lewis, 1898-1963
British writer, Literary scholar and
Anglican lay theologian

7.4 Legal Ramifications of Intervention

What are the legal ramifications of intervening? Knowing *how* to intervene is the second hurdle. Before taking action to intervene with or terminate a depressed employee, managers should be aware of applicable federal, state and local anti-discrimination and disability laws. Such laws are typically designed to protect people with disabilities who are otherwise qualified and able to perform the essential functions of their jobs.

When is a resignation not a resignation? This is the question that managers or leaders ought to be asking if the resignation follows a period of performance management, or an employee has a mental illness or other debilitating condition at the time.

An employee made an unfair dismissal claim against an Australian company which the company sought to have struck out on the basis that the employee had, in fact, resigned.

The employee had a history of depression which raised itself in performance issues as well as assertions that the employee had been intimidating other employees. On the basis of these allegations, which were proven along with recommendations from the company's EAP psychologist, the employee was given the option of moving to another office 32 kms away for three months.

The employee took sick leave and lodged a worker's compensation claim before reluctantly returning to work in the other office. A further incident occurred, a disciplinary enquiry was initiated, and the employee was asked to respond in writing, upon which the employee again went on sick leave. While on sick leave, the company sent the employee an email reminding her that on her first day back she would need to respond in relation to the disciplinary enquiry. She replied via email that she would not be returning to work as per her attached medical certificate which stated that she was "unable to return to her current workplace". Her supervisor asked her if this meant that she was resigning, to which the employee said "Yes".

After a close look at events leading up to the resignation, and the circumstances in which it was given, the Australian Industrial Relations Commission (AIRC) decided that the employee had not resigned voluntarily, but was forced to do so because of the company's conduct.

The implications for employers are that they should:

* Be careful about requiring a response to misconduct allegations or resuming a performance process immediately upon an employee's return from sick leave.

* Not assume an employee has resigned if they say they cannot return to work (e.g., due to medical reasons), particularly if they are not in the right frame of mind at the time. The employee may need to be given time to properly consider their position.

* Provide a copy of any report (e.g., medical, OH&S consultant or psychologist) relied on in making decisions affecting an employee (unless there are exceptional circumstances), and seek the employee's response.

* Ensure temporary arrangements are just that – temporary. If they are designed to address workplace conflict or other performance issues, put steps in place to address the underlying concerns.

In general, employers cannot discriminate against people with disabilities in any and all phases of work, including pre-hiring, hiring, employment and termination. Many laws are designed to assist employees who desire, **what is called an "accommodation"**[1] in order to continue working, or to protect

---

[1] In the context of employment law, "accommodation" refers to a legal requirement for employers to make adjustments or modifications to the work environment or job duties in order to enable employees with certain disabilities or medical conditions to continue working or to be considered for employment. These accommodations are designed to ensure that employees with disabilities have equal opportunities in the workplace and are not discriminated against based on their disability. Examples of accommodations include providing a flexible work schedule, modifying job duties or responsibilities, making changes to the physical layout of the

them when a conditional offer of employment – subject to a physical examination – is made.

7.4.1 Legal Issues to Consider

To protect the organisation against anti-discrimination lawsuits, managers, HR professional and employee assistance providers should be able to answer the following general questions. These questions provide guide-posts as to how to operate:

- Is the worker qualified to do the job or not?

- Does the worker have a disability which, without a reasonable accommodation, will prevent them from performing?

- Have you attempted to make reasonable accommodations so that the worker can perform their job responsibilities?

- Have you taken care to protect the employee's right to confidentiality? Employers must keep all information concerning the medical condition or psychiatric history of its applicants or employees confidential.

- Have you properly documented conversations, interviews and actions taken?

---

workplace, providing assistive devices or technologies, allowing for telecommuting or remote work, modifying policies or procedures, or providing additional breaks or time off for medical appointments or treatments.

7.4.1.1 Substantial Limitation

The primary legal question you need to answer is this: *Is the worker disabled?* Generally, the worker's impairment rises to the level of disability if it "substantially limits" performance. Substantial limitation is evaluated in terms of the severity of the limitation and the length of time it restricts performance. Substantial limitation is generally defined as lasting for several months and significantly restricting the performance.

Example A:
An employee has had clinical depression for almost a year. He has been intensely sad and socially withdrawn (except for going to work), has developed serious insomnia, and has had severe problems concentrating. The impairment – clinical depression – significantly restricts his ability to interact with others, sleep, and concentrate. The impairment is severe and has lasted long enough to be substantially limiting.

Some conditions are considered to be disabilities if they are long-term or potentially long-term, in that their duration is indefinite, unknowable or is expected to last several months.

Example B:
An employee has taken medication for bipolar disorder for several months. For some time before starting medication, he experienced increasingly severe and frequent cycles of depression and mania; at times he became extremely withdrawn or had difficulty caring for himself. His symptoms have abated with medication, but his doctor says that the duration and course of his bipolar disorder is indefinite, although it is potentially long-term. The impairment – bipolar disorder –

significantly restricts his ability to interact with others and care for himself, when considered without medication.

Conditions that are temporary and have no permanent or long-term effects on an individual's major life activities are not substantially limiting.

Example C:

An employee was distressed by the end of a romantic relationship. Although he continued his daily routine, he sometimes became agitated at work. He was most distressed for about a month during and immediately after the breakup. He sought counselling, and his mood improved within weeks. His counsellor stated that he was not expected to experience any permanent or long-term problems associated with this event. This employee does not have a disability.

Most disability laws do not consider traits or behaviours to be, in themselves, mental impairments. For example, stress, in itself, is not automatically a mental impairment. Traits like irritability, chronic lateness, and poor judgment are not, in themselves, mental impairments.

It's important to be aware that some courts have found that individuals may not need to establish a psychiatric disability to show that they're substantially limited in working. For example, they may have trouble sleeping, concentrating, or caring for themselves.

7.4.1.2 The Role of Medication in Substantial Limitation

Should the corrective effects of medication be considered when deciding whether an impairment is so severe that it substantially limits the worker? No. An individual who is taking medication for depression may be considered to have a disability if there is evidence that the mental impairment, when left untreated, substantially limits work performance. It may be important to document an individual's condition before starting medication and how an individual's condition changed when they went off medication or had dosages adjusted.

7.4.1.3 Are Job Applicants Required to Disclose Psychiatric History and Disabilities?

No. An employer may generally not ask questions that are likely to elicit information about a disability (including psychiatric disability) before making a job offer. However, if an applicant voluntarily asks for a reasonable accommodation during the hiring process, the employer may require the applicant to provide documentation from an appropriate health care professional concerning the disability and functional limitations.

7.4.1.4 Can an Employer Require a Medical or Psychiatric Examination of an Employee?

In general, yes, if a disability-related inquiry or medical examination of an employee is job-related and consistent with business necessity. The employer must have evidence that:

1. An employee's ability to perform essential job functions will be impaired by a medical condition.

2. An employee will pose a direct threat due to a medical condition.

Example A:
A limousine service is aware that one of its drivers has bipolar disorder and had a manic episode the

previous year while driving a customer. During the manic episode, the chauffeur engaged in repeated behaviour in which he drove a company limousine in a reckless manner, posing a direct threat to himself and others. In this regard, it is reasonable for an employer to request a psychiatric examination to determine the suitability of the employee for the position.

Example B:

An employee with clinical depression wishes to return to work after a leave of absence during which she was hospitalised and her medication was adjusted. Her employer may request a fitness-for-duty examination because there is a reasonable belief that her ability to perform essential job functions may continue to be impaired. The examination, however, must be limited to the effect of her depression on her ability, with or without reasonable accommodation, to perform essential job functions. She is not required to reveal her entire psychiatric history.

7.4.1.5 When Do Problems with Others Amount to a Substantial Limitation?

When the impaired person is significantly restricted from interacting with others productively, as compared to the average person in the general population, there is evidence of a substantial limitation. So, for example, unfriendliness with co-workers or a supervisor is not sufficient to establish a substantial limitation. However, it can be established if an individual regularly has severe problems with others, such as consistently high levels of hostility, social withdrawal, or failure to communicate when necessary.

7.4.1.6 Inquiries from Co-workers

How should an employer respond when employees ask questions about a co-worker who has a disability? The employer must not disclose any medical information about an employee, or tell other employees whether it is providing a reasonable accommodation for a particular individual.

Chapter 7 Summary

The "**Rule of Five**" says that you need to be aware of any employee who complains of five or more symptoms or physical complaints, because the possibility of them having an underlying mental disorder (including depression) is highly likely.

Research shows that clinical depression is the *most frequent* diagnosis associated with **absence from the workplace**. It is also responsible for more **missed days at work** (709 per 1,000 employees) than other condition. So, these are two obvious signs. There are also other tell-tale signs (withdrawn, conflict with other workers, etc).

How do you decide to step in and intervene? Many employers want to respond compassionately to employee health problems, but managers walk a fine line with employees. When is personal *too* personal?

Generally, one should intervene when the employee becomes a management problem, when there is an obvious performance problem, or when one has reason to believe the employee may be at risk for suicide. Screening for depression can be a matter of simply asking two questions:

1. *"Over the past two weeks, have you felt down, depressed, or hopeless?"*

2. *"Have you felt little interest or pleasure in doing things?"*

Alternatively, several formal screening tools are available.

Before taking action to intervene with or terminate a depressed employee, managers should be aware of applicable federal, state or local anti-discrimination and disability laws. In general, employers cannot discriminate against people with disabilities in any and all phases of work, including pre-hiring, hiring, employment and termination.

Many laws are designed to assist employees who desire an "accommodation" in order to continue working, or to protect them when a conditional offer of employment – subject to a physical examination – is made.

"It's so difficult to describe depression to someone who's never been there because it's not sadness."

J.K. Rowling, 1965-
British Author and Philanthropist

CHAPTER 8

Be Preventative and Proactive:
Set the Culture for Managing a Depressed Employee

Introduction

If you don't manage workplace depression, it will manage you.

Most employers and companies are not very effective when it comes to health care issues, particularly mental health care issues. Sure they know how to manufacture "widgets" or distribute "goods" or sell "stuff", but they are not savvy about mental health care. Those that are, are the exception, not the rule.

Given the high cost of workplace depression, having in place an aggressive, proactive program for identifying and treating depression has become both good medical practice and good business practice. The challenge for employers is clear: How do you halt the ripple effects of workplace depression?

The solution is: Managing depressed employees, both as a group and one at a time.

Prevention and recovery is a partnership. Hence, all parties must work toward the same goals: Having proactive programs and restoring the depressive to the workplace in good health.

Supervisors and HR professionals can't "fix" a depressed employee. Nor is it their job to make a diagnosis. However, they can provide educational programs, offer positive, non-judgmental, practical support, and connect the employee to the necessary resources and mental health professionals.

Such programs have a direct benefit to a company's bottom line. A recent study by Dr. Philip Wang (formerly of Harvard University and now director of NIMH's Division of Services and Intervention Research) was conducted with 604 employees who were enrolled in a managed behavioural health care plan.[1] All of the employees were identified as having clinically significant depression during web-based and telephone screening processes. The treatment group was offered telephone support from a care manager and their choice of telephone psychotherapy, in-person therapy or anti-depressant medication. The control group was offered "usual care", which was feedback about their screening results and advice to seek help from their usual source.

After twelve months, employees in the treatment group were 40% more likely to have recovered from their depression compared to those in usual care, and were also 70% more likely to stay employed, as well as working an average of two more hours per week than those in usual care.

Importantly for employers too, the study noted that the value of more hours worked among those in the treatment group who were employed was estimated at $1,800 per employee per year, which far exceeded the $100-$400 per person cost associated with the type of outreach provided for the treatment group.

The conclusion was that systematic efforts to identify and treat depression in the workplace significantly improved employee health and productivity, leading to lower costs overall for the employer.[1]

8.1 Laying the Foundation: The Keys to Effective Depression Management

8.1.1 What are the Obstacles to Effective Depression Management?

Businesses tend to design day-to-day productivity plans around the optimal workplace: Everyone will show up for work, everyone will be healthy, and everyone will be productive. But it just doesn't work like that. Unfortunately for most companies, it is rarely the case that these expectations of everything going smoothly are actually met. *Thanks to depression (among other things), someone either doesn't show up, or shows up unhealthy and is unproductive.*

It's human nature, though, to keep going. Most of us are not good at being sick – we don't know how to be sick. Depressed employees usually don't know whether they need treatment, don't know how to go about receiving it, and are afraid to explore the possibilities.

Depressives tend to be their own worst enemies, which is another reason it's often necessary for managers to intervene.

One of the main barriers to managing depression is the general ignorance and lack of knowledge about depression itself.

Firstly, a major national survey conducted in 2007 by Beyond Blue in Australia showed, for example, that there was a **lack of understanding about the types of behaviour which may be helpful or unhelpful for someone with depression.**[2] For instance, over half the sample indicated that *"It would be helpful to encourage someone with depression to take time off work or go on a holiday."* Sadly, all this really does is give the mind more time to stalk its victim! Time on your hands when you're depressed can send you into a spiral. If anything, time off work might mean that it's harder to get back to the workplace, which is obviously to the detriment of the individual as well as to the organisation.

Secondly, there was **a lack of certainty about helpful strategies to assist someone who may be experiencing depression in the workplace**. The survey found that over 10% of professionals suggested it would be *"helpful to take someone with depression out to the pub for a few drinks to help them forget their worries"*. This kind of action though, could well compound the problem and make the situation worse.

Less than half (46%) of the professionals in this national survey indicated that they thought it would be *"helpful to suggest that someone in their workplace try to get hold of some self-help materials"*, and 44% indicated that it was probably *"unhelpful to follow someone up and make sure that they got professional help"*. While both of these strategies for depressed persons can be very helpful, the professionals surveyed were not sufficiently confident to recommend such tactics.

In organisations in which workplace depression occurs, **employee surveys** also reveal common obstacles to seeking treatment and help:

- The stigma that employees believe will be associated with an official diagnosis or label; no one wants to be stigmatised

- The belief that such might be career limiting, in that a diagnosis may affect their career path and chances of promotion

- Lack of motivation to seek care because they're ashamed to need care and not confident of treatment success

- Ignorance about available treatment options and the benefits of treatment

- Lack of confidence in the employee's doctors or EAP professionals

- Local doctors are not adequately trained in mental health care

- Concerns about privacy and confidentiality

8.1.2 Building the Depression Management Plan – Where Do You Start?

You start by removing the obstacles. The most important first steps employers can take are practical ones.

1. Communicate your confidentiality policy and enforce it.

One-quarter of Americans say they would be concerned about privacy if their employer's human resources department found out they were seeing a mental health professional.[3]

You've probably heard the saying, "Our organisation leaks like a sieve". This is what most employees fear – gossip, rumour, innuendo, and a situation in which nothing is private and everyone seems to know everyone else's business. This is what we all hate and fear.

Make the policy clear and publicise it. Make sure that it's not just words on paper. Companies and businesses are full of policies that are nothing more than nice sounding words that do not play out in the behaviour or the culture of the organisation. And everyone knows it.

Reassure employees up front that any conversation with line supervisors, managers, HR professionals, employee assistance providers, representatives, personnel counsellors, internal coaches, or treating professionals will remain confidential.

It's one thing to have a policy, it's another to enforce it. Any infringement of any kind in relation to a break in confidentiality needs to be dealt with, and publicly so. Even if the infringement of confidentiality is based on hearsay, act on it. "Cut it off at the pass", as they say. Even if the hearsay led to nothing, it doesn't matter. You showed that you were serious about apparent breaches. It only takes one infringement that goes unchecked for everyone to get the message that your organisation doesn't walk the talk.

2. **Educate employees about the symptoms of depression and the importance of seeking treatment.**

    Education, as in all things, can be the silver bullet in the battle against workplace depression.

    Providing easy access to depression resources can help counter the stigma of depression and give employees a sense of empowerment. Knowledge helps depressed workers achieve a greater sense of control over their circumstances and start to shift out of negative-thinking mode and into problem-solving mode.

    Examples of employee awareness and education strategies include:

    - Distributing **brochures** that challenge the myths associated with depression.

    - Ensuring that at **staff orientation sessions** the material on depression is covered and understood. If orientation is via an intranet, ensure that candidates have ticked the section on mental illness or have even passed a brief test on what they have learned before they can proceed further.

- Offering **workshops** that foster emotional well-being and team-building, and making such workshops mandatory and not just for those few who probably know the material anyway.

- Assembling a **task force** charged with creating a workplace environment that is supportive.

- Building a depression **resources library** — books, audio-books, videos, intranet and internet websites.

3. **Offer depression screenings or other early detection programs.**

Depression screenings can include formal tests such as the Beck Depression Inventory, or psychologist and primary care doctor assessments, as well as a confidential self-referral system.

The U.S. Occupational Safety and Health Administration's Employee Assistance Program offers its member employers a confidential Employee Telephone Access Program. This interactive, computerised system allows employees and their families to take a free, anonymous self-test for depression via a toll-free number. The program provides immediate test results and doctor referrals specifically provided by their company. Employers, managed-care corporations, EAP consultants and unions can register to have this service administered within their organisation.[3]

There was a major national initiative launched in Australia in which an independent, not-for-profit organisation called *Beyond Blue* was set up, originally funded by federal and state governments for five years from 2000 to 2005 but now has been providing services for over 20 years.

Prior to that, there was no national recognition of the work that had been undertaken in the field of depression, and there was no coordinated or unified national approach to tackling depressive disorders. This initiative moved the focus of depression away from a mental health service issue to one which was acknowledged and addressed by the wider community.

Not surprisingly, there are depression checklists available on the site to assess your level of depression:
(https://www.beyondblue.org.au/the-facts/mental-health-check-in-k10).

Early detection means early treatment, which increases the odds of a shorter recovery period and decreases the odds of recurrence. In an occupational setting, the early goals of the mental health professional are to:

- Understand the main complaints
- Examine potential causes
- Reach a preliminary diagnosis

4. **Offer employees access to outpatient care and a broad spectrum of services, settings, and providers.**

    Build a comprehensive provider network, from employee assistance professionals to local doctors, psychologists and psychiatrists. Make sure that employees thoroughly understand your health care system (either through the company itself or through available government and private health schemes), and know how to maximise their treatment options and insurance benefits.

5. **Develop a return-to-work or re-entry plan for employees who have been absent due to depression.**

    Your ultimate goal is for depressed employees to return to work healthy, productive and able to manage their depression. Re-entry and return-to-work plans are generally graduated, meaning the employee returns for, say, three days a week for a month, then four days for a further period, etc., before returning full time.

    Create a culture of support. For example, you can assign an empathetic liaison person who can be trusted to listen non-judgmentally to the employee's concerns. Perhaps there could be a liaison in HR who follows up regularly.

    Don't be afraid to follow up with the occasional friendly inquiry about how the person is doing. It's important that depressives don't feel like the rug has been pulled out from under them once they've been discharged by their therapist. Support is a key element in both preventing escalation of symptoms and conquering recurrent depression.

6. Develop clear guidelines for job flexibility and accommodations.

Often, reasonable "accommodations" and modifications can be offered to a depressed worker for little effort and at little or no cost (see also Section 7.4 in Chapter 7 regarding "accommodations").

Accommodations come in many forms, from changes in a supervisor's communication style to job modifications or physical changes to the work environment.

Sometimes it's just a matter of flexibility. For example, offer the depressed employee a flexible schedule that allows them to participate in therapy and other mental health support programs or allow an employee with poor physical stamina to extend their shifts in order to take additional rest breaks during the day. In general, the best outcome is achieved when employees are given a sense of control over the way they manage time and do their job.

Whenever feasible, remove workplace stressors that create chronic strain and contribute to the employee's depression, such as co-worker conflict. Supervisors who become actively involved in resolving conflicts and improving morale and working conditions can have a significant impact on both employee health and workplace health.

Other examples of reasonable accommodations include:

- Reassuring an employee who is re-entering the work force after a long psychiatric hospitalisation, and having supervisors be sure to include positive feedback along with performance monitoring.

- For an employee who needs a clear time structure and clear productivity goals, schedule planning sessions each morning.

- If an employee is struggling with certain job tasks, exchange those with another employee's tasks.

- For an employee who is having difficulty concentrating in an open work area, install a partition or room divider.

7. Develop a critical incident response strategy.

Don't wait for a crisis to strike. Have a rapid response strategy in place before you need one. (See Chapter 13 for more resources for managing a severe depressive episode in the workplace.)

8. Train managers to identify, manage and assist employees with depression.

In many cases, observant managers will be the early detection mechanism, and perhaps the interveners.

The GRO-DOH model, which will be discussed in the next chapter, provides managers with a practical, but comprehensive strategy for intervention. GRO-DOH is designed to help managers structure a conversation with an employee about their mood, behaviour or performance.

Run a workshop for all supervisors, to educate them not only about the signs and symptoms of depression, but also about how to intervene, what to say, and when. The GRO-DOH model in the next chapter will assist with this step.

8.2 Learn From Others

You don't have to reinvent the wheel. And you don't have to spend a small fortune to build an effective depression management program. Studying other successful programs can help you implement your own.

To date, the main thrust for programs has come from health benefit companies that see that there is a market for their products and services (e.g., in the U.S., there is Aetna's Depression Management Initiative, and CIGNA's Well Aware Depression Management Program and in Australia there is Beyond Blue).

When designing your depression management program, be sure to involve all the principals or stakeholders, including:
- Human resources professionals
- Local doctor
- Psychologists, psychiatrists, and other mental health professionals
- Occupational health and safety professionals

- Corporate attorneys or commercial lawyers
- Key supervisors or managers
- Health plan administrators and policy-makers
- Representatives of trade unions and other employee organisations
- Insurance company representatives
- Employees

Don't forget to involve employees in the solution. Employees may turn out to be your single most valuable source of information. Remember, too, that they need to take ownership of the program, and that including them in the consultation process is an important step. Strategies for gleaning information might include:

- Holding meetings or focus groups with groups of employees
- Distributing questionnaires or surveys to gather opinions
- Asking for and encouraging feedback
- Establishing an information booth in the company cafeteria, placing a suggestion box in the staff room, or creating an information hotline
- Conducting one-on-one interviews with key employees and randomly selected employees

Don't forget to monitor progress. You may find it useful to select a **special task force** of individuals to monitor the welfare of employees and recommend strategies for promoting mental health. This way the project doesn't get lost or forgotten. The task force can compile feedback from employees and compare notes about the quality of the organisation's mental health education, treatments and insurance benefits, as well as the general quality of life in the workplace. They can also explore team relationships and overall workplace morale and motivation levels.

A dynamic, ongoing system such as this helps organisations adapt and react to small problems before they become big problems.

"Depression is being colour-blind and constantly told how colourful the world is."

Atticus,
British Canadian anonymous poet

Chapter 8 Summary

Prevention is better than cure, especially when it goes straight to the bottom line and reduces absenteeism and low productivity. If a cure is required, employers need to know what to do in a timely manner, and not at the actual point of crisis, when poor decisions are often made.

Employers and companies are encouraged to implement a comprehensive depression management program, the core of which would entail the following:

- Initiation of stress management and depression education programs to increase disease awareness among employees

- Education of supervisors to recognize the signs and symptoms of depression

- Encouragement of employees to contact trained employee assistance program personnel for referrals for diagnosis and treatment

- Assurance that depression identification and education are integral parts of every health care initiative undertaken within the company

---

"Hiding in my room, safe within my womb,
I touch no one and no one touches me.
I am a rock, I am an island.
And a rock feels no pain;
And an island never cries."

Paul Simon, 1941-
American singer-songwriter
(From the song, "I am a Rock")

CHAPTER 9

GRO-DOH:
A Comprehensive Model for Manager Intervention

Introduction

Before you get into a conversation with a depressed employee, you need to think about what you want to say. Typically, however, most managers are stressed about such conversations fearing that somehow, they might make matters worse. *"What if I stuff it up?" "What if they cry or get angry?" "What if they storm off?" "What if they simply won't talk?" "What if they say it's nothing really and they're ok?" "What if I push them over the edge?"*

Not surprisingly, many managers just hope that the problem will go away and they put off or procrastinate about such conversations. Part of the problem is that they don't know how to start the discussion and have no real plan about how to handle the conversation.

Furthermore, there's little point in winging it, or just seeing how it goes. That's probably a recipe for disaster. You owe it to yourself and your staff member to do better than that.

It is therefore important that you have a formula for the conversation and that you don't get lost, ramble or get off target or get flustered and forget what you're really saying. Instead, you need to have a structure to which you adhere. It's a sure safety net for yourself as well as the employee.

Both planning before the conversation what you wish to say, **plus** having a structure for the conversation sets you up for success in the interaction.

9.1 Preparing for a Discussion about the Issue

Preparing your presentation of an issue helps prevent incoherent or incomplete explanations of the problem. Spend time thinking about it. We're all busy, and managers sometimes complain that there's never enough time, but good managers find time to think.

If you don't have ten minutes to spare for something this important, then it could be that you're headed for burn-out and depression too! Put aside the time; you're less likely to make mistakes under pressure during the conversation, and it will calm your nerves.

There's a saying you may have heard that goes, "Fail to plan and you plan to fail". Wise words.

Your employees appreciate good use of their time, too. At the top of that list is the accurate identification of a problem.

Let's go through the steps of thinking through the issue, and preparing ourselves for the discussion.

1. The issue is:
Be concise. In one or two sentences, get to the heart of the problem. Is it a concern, challenge, or recurring problem that is becoming more troublesome? Don't waffle. Be specific.

2. It is significant because:
What's at stake? How does this affect morale, dollars, income, people, products, services, customers, family, timing, the future, or other relevant factors? Importantly, what is the future impact if the issue is not resolved? What would happen if this situation continued? Where would you or the team [department, company] be in X period of time if this was allowed to go on?

3. The ideal outcome is:
What specific results do you want?

4. Relevant background information:
Summarise with bulleted points: How, when, why, and where did the issue start? Who are the key players? Which forces are at work? What is the issue's current status?

5. What have you done up to this point:
What have you done so far? (e.g., observed the staff member, heard rumours consistently over a number of weeks, made notes, kept examples of mistakes or poor work). What options are you considering?

6. What help do you want from the staff member:
What participation do you expect from the staff member? (e.g., alternative solutions, identification of consequences, where to find more information, or agreement on a treatment plan).

9.2 Having a GRO-DOH Conversation

What is GRO-DOH? This is an acronym for a model devised by the author that allows managers and leaders to have a structured conversation with the troubled employee. It is a roadmap for the actual discussion. It shows where to start, how to progress, and how to bring it to a conclusion.[1]

The letters in GRO-DOH stand for the six parts of the conversation that you need to attend to in order to make sure that you have covered all the aspects of the issue with the employee.

G = Goal of the conversation

R = Reality of the current situation

O = Options to consider

D = Direct action to take

O = Obstacles that might get in the way

H = Homework and follow-up

Let's explore each part of this model and each part of this conversation, which is shown in diagram form on the next page.

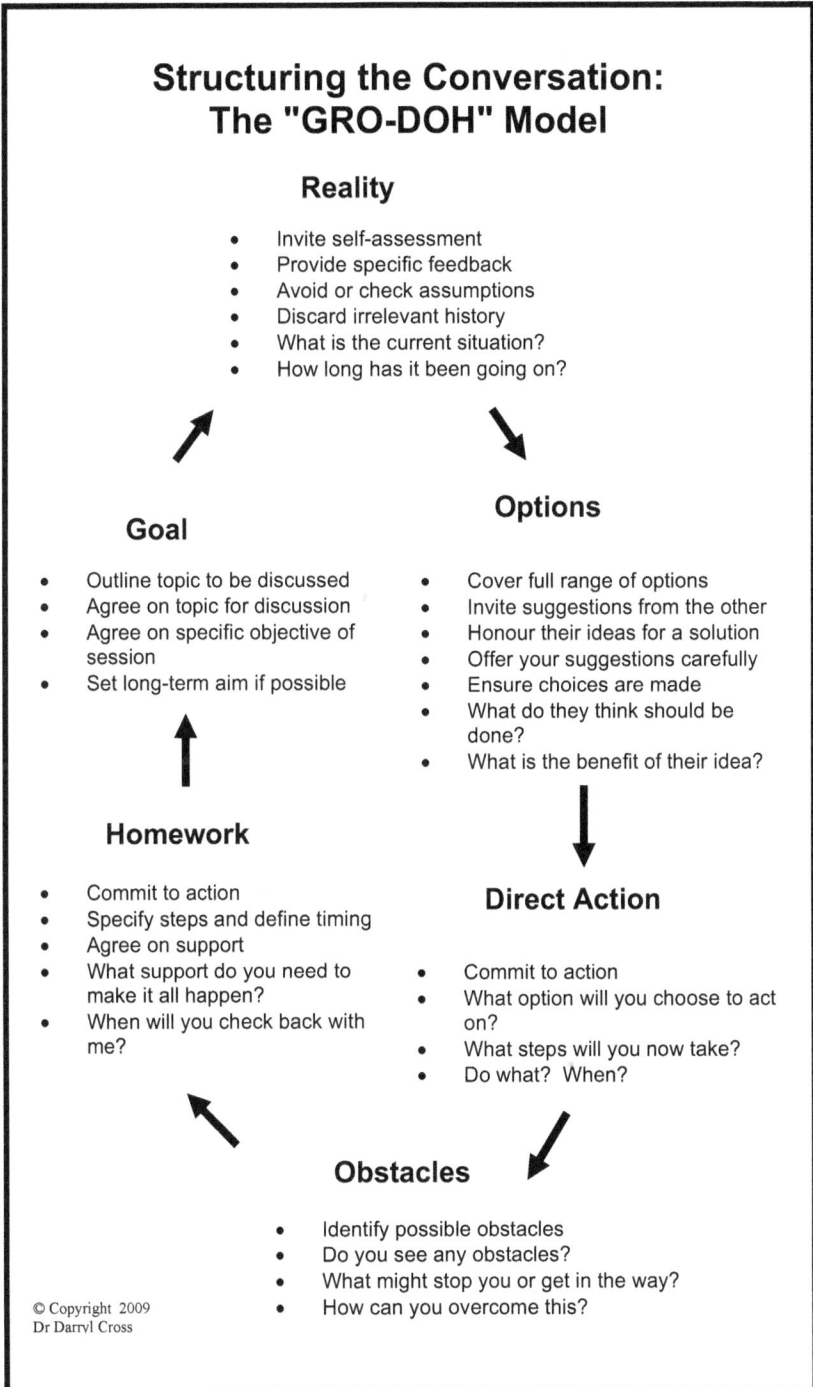

Figure 9.1

Structuring the Conversation:
The "GRO-DOH" Model

Reality

- Invite self-assessment
- Provide specific feedback
- Avoid or check assumptions
- Discard irrelevant history
- What is the current situation?
- How long has it been going on?

Goal

- Outline topic to be discussed
- Agree on topic for discussion
- Agree on specific objective of session
- Set long-term aim if possible

Options

- Cover full range of options
- Invite suggestions from the other
- Honour their ideas for a solution
- Offer your suggestions carefully
- Ensure choices are made
- What do they think should be done?
- What is the benefit of their idea?

Homework

- Commit to action
- Specify steps and define timing
- Agree on support
- What support do you need to make it all happen?
- When will you check back with me?

Direct Action

- Commit to action
- What option will you choose to act on?
- What steps will you now take?
- Do what? When?

Obstacles

- Identify possible obstacles
- Do you see any obstacles?
- What might stop you or get in the way?
- How can you overcome this?

© Copyright 2009
Dr Darryl Cross

Goal

Outline the topic to be discussed. Set a clear goal, if at all possible. Note that you may have to come back to the goal during the discussion to make it really clear. Set an objective for the session.

Possible questions or statements:

"What I'd like to discuss is...
> *...that you don't seem to be enthusiastic about your work any more."*
> *...that you seem very tired and fatigued now."*
> *...the fact that you've been late to work three times over the last week."*
> *...the fact that you've missed two deadlines in a row now and set back the team's schedule."*
> *...the fact that you've been absent from work four times over the last month."*
> *...that I've observed you becoming quite hostile in meetings in a way that I've not witnessed before."*
> *...that you're not participating in meetings at all like you were previously and, in fact, at times you say nothing."*

Reality

Discuss specific details about what is happening, when it happens, and what solutions have been tried so far. The staff member needs to come to a better understanding of the situation, which will help them develop options and solutions.

Possible questions or statements:

"Given what I've said already, how do you see the situation?"
"What's the situation as you see it? Can you tell me more about that?"
"On a scale of 1-10, where are you now (where 1 = poor/ awful and 10 = outstanding/excellent)"
"What is happening at the moment?"
"How do you know that this is accurate?"
"When does this happen? How often?"
"What effect does this have?"
"How have you, or how could you, verify that?"
"How do others see this situation?"
"What other factors are relevant?"
"What have you tried? What worked?"

Options

List solutions that might work. Get the staff member to come up with solutions. Find out what has worked for them in other situations or what they have seen work for others. Getting them to come up with solutions first means that you get greater buy-in from them. This is very important. They may also have a solution that you haven't thought of as yet.

Possible questions or statements:

"What other options do you have? What else could you do?"
"How can we get there? How could you move to an 8 (from a 3 or 4 or whatever)?"
"What are all the possible actions that you can see?"

"Are there times when the problem does not occur? What's different about those situations?"
"How have you stopped the problem from completely overwhelming you?"
"What has worked for you in the past?"
"What are some potential pitfalls?"
"What support do you need to make it happen?"
"What would have to happen to make it work?"
"What option will you choose to act on?"
"If you woke up tomorrow morning and the problem had disappeared and everything was as you'd like it to be, what would that be like?"
"If you had a friend in this kind of situation, what would you suggest to them?"

Direct Action

From these options, develop an action plan – small steps they can easily take that will lead to the solution. It's a good idea to write out the action plan. Writing it out helps it feel more concrete and more real, and chances are that the depressed person may not remember what you've discussed unless you commit it to paper or to the keyboard.

Possible questions or statements:

"What are the next steps?"
"You'll do what? By when?"
"Precisely when will you take them?"
"What support will you need?"
"What will you do to get the support you need to move along?"

Obstacles

Make sure the staff member feels confident that they can actually complete the action plan. This is where it can all break down. Like many others, the staff member may be well-intentioned, but not follow through. As I've said before, *"Life rewards actions, not good intentions"*. This is a critical step; overlook it at your peril.

Possible questions or statements:

"Do you see any obstacles here?"
"What might stop you or get in the way of you achieving
 your next step? How can you overcome this?"
"How will you know that you're on track for success?"
"How can I help you in moving forward?"

Homework

This is the point at which you confirm what they are going to do and arrange a time to follow-up. As the manager or leader, you need to stay in touch with what is happening. Even if the agreement is that the staff member will seek professional help, you need to stay informed. You don't need to know the details of the professional's diagnosis, prognosis or treatment, but you do need to verify that the depressed staff member made an appointment, kept the appointment, and continues to consult with the professional.

Possible questions or statements:

"Is there anything else that needs to be covered?"
"Now let's just make sure that we know what we're going to
 do."

"Let's go over what we planned to do."
"Can we make arrangements for our next meeting?"
"When would it be convenient to meet again?"
"Given what your game plan is, how about we set
      an appointment for about two weeks from now."

9.3 What Are the Advantages of the GRO-DOH Model?

As has been indicated, this framework gives the manager or leader a roadmap for how to conduct those discussions that typically managers worry about and sometimes avoid, in the hope that it all might go away. This is a way of providing support to the employee as well as giving the manager a framework to follow.

A **proforma sheet** has already been prepared for leaders and managers to use showing the six headings and possible questions to ask, as well as providing space to write notes and a space at the end to summarise the conversation and make notes in preparation for the next meeting. This template can be downloaded from the Resources tab at **www.drdarryl.com**. It is important to emphasise that you need to take notes during these conversations – this is sound HR practice – and this proforma allows you to do so.

Experience shows that having these structured conversations on a regular basis (e.g., weekly or fortnightly) means that either one of two things will occur.

The **first** possibility is that the individual will change their behaviour and take steps to remedy their situation. In this case, GRO-DOH serves to ensure that they remain on track. You can have a GRO-DOH conversation with the depressed staff member perhaps every two to three weeks as a way of supporting them and ensuring that they stay on track.

It will be fairly easy for them to take a first step to bring about change (e.g., see their local doctor for a referral to a psychiatrist, or see an EAP counsellor), but to actually follow through and remain committed to their continued growth and change is another matter. Many people can take the first step, but not everyone remains committed.

Bear in mind that genuine change, in which someone begins to form new habits, usually takes a minimum of six months. As in getting fit, one trip to the gym won't do the trick. Consistently working out at the gym a number of times each week will result in some initial change after about a month, and substantial results after about three months. After six months, the body is fit, but the individual still needs to maintain those good habits to stay fit.

It's the same with mental health. Good things take time. Good mental health habits don't happen with one visit to the psychologist. Regular visits (e.g., every two weeks to monthly) are what is required to really change around thought patterns and ways of behaving and reacting. It's the same in the workplace. Make sure that the GRO-DOH conversations occur at least every two weeks (if not weekly), depending on the situation, until the staff member becomes more independent and more effective, and change has occurred.

The **second** possible outcome from using the GRO-DOH model on a regular basis, is that the staff member will be resistant to change or decide that the job, the career or the culture is not for them. They have thought through the issues with you and discussed the options. Typically, they will then resign.

Sometimes employees don't like looking in the mirror in the way that GRO-DOH encourages them to do. They would rather escape than have to face the realities of who they are and how they are behaving. We can only hope that at some point they will be prepared to face their issues and try to work through them.

These kinds of discussions allow the employee time to think and appraise the situation, probably in a way that they have not done before. Such structured conversations show respect for the employee. Perhaps no one has taken the time to be a sounding board for them in such a way. Through these discussions, they may come to certain realisations and understandings about their life and their career, and they may choose to move on.

Sometimes, it might mean too that they gain career direction and look at other avenues that might be available and that suit them better, or they decide to look at particular courses or study that is available. GRO-DOH gives employees the opportunity to consider what they really wish to do. Importantly, it allows staff to take responsibility for their own careers and their own lives.

Chapter 9 Summary

Managers need a model to use in order to discuss the situation with a depressed employee. Such a conversation can be anxiety-provoking for supervisors and leaders for a number of reasons.

GRO-DOH is an excellent model to use for structuring the conversation. It has been adopted by many leaders because it works.

GRO-DOH gives managers and leaders an effective way to supportively assist employees who are depressed and who are struggling.

"My recovery from manic depression has been an evolution, not a sudden miracle."

Patty Duke, 1946-
American actress

CHAPTER 10

The Non-Compliant Employee

Introduction

As the manager or leader, you have a plan. You know how to help the depressed employee, and in the process improve productivity and reduce health care costs. However, you've heard the expression taken from a Robert Burns poem: *"The best laid plans of mice and men often go awry"*.

Suppose the employee doesn't comply with your plan? Some employees may refuse assistance. Others may accept assistance, but then abandon treatment before recovery has been achieved.

The most common forms of non-compliance are:
- **Denial** that depression exists
    "What are you talking about, I don't have depression!"
    "Doesn't everyone have a down day now and again?"

- **Medication non-compliance**
  "Some days I just forget to take it."
  "You know I hate taking drugs."

- **Therapy non-compliance**
  "What do doctors know anyway?"
  "You can't always trust what they say, you know."

Let's look at each of these in more detail.

10.1 Depression Denial

Be prepared for depressed employees to be in denial. Many will be, especially at first. Accepting that one has a disorder is painful. Accepting that something is wrong is not easy.

The employee may shrug it off, or explain away their symptoms: *"I'm fine – I've just felt a little tired lately. The baby keeps me up all night"*. They may concoct a false, minor medical problem: *"I think it must be my allergies making me a little off-colour"*.

Depressives typically know how to fool people, but they don't know how to get their own needs met. Their psychological defence mechanisms may be so strong that they become experts at fooling people, and may be able to fool themselves as well, since many depressives are out of touch with their own emotions and feelings. A depressive usually won't communicate the depth of their pain and fear. They may fear you will reject them, and that there will be negative career consequences if they admit to this affliction.

How should you handle the depressive in denial? The GRO-DOH model in Chapter 9 will help you find the right way to talk to the employee. You'll recall that GRO-DOH provides a model for a structured conversation. It provides a clear roadmap for how to bring up the topic, and then how to move forward in the conversation in such a way that you cover all the bases, and yet allow room for the person to maintain their autonomy and provide options or solutions as necessary.

GRO-DOH is effective when there is clear evidence that the employee's work performance has deteriorated (e.g., late for work, missing deadlines, absenteeism, making numerous mistakes, or overlooking important details). It is difficult for the depressive to deny the obvious facts. They might try, but you are prepared to quietly re-assert the obvious. For example:

- *"I've noticed that you've been late to work almost every day for the past week or so."*

- *"Lately, you seem to be more prone to making mistakes."*

- *"Lately, it seems to take you longer to get your work done."*

Alternatively, you may need to orchestrate a gentle intervention − structure your conversation in such a way that you lead up to the topic of depression more gradually, gently. It may not even be necessary to mention the word "depression", per se. You can frame your observations in the context of the employee's demeanour, their apparent sluggishness, and the fact that they just seem down and not with it. For example:

- *"Lately, you seem to be having difficulty concentrating."*

- *"You don't look like you've been sleeping well."*

- *"You don't seem to be very enthusiastic about your job anymore."*

Employees may very well deny their depression, but not deny their poor performance or their apparent low mood and fatigue. If you **pinpoint performance issues** as your reason for referring them to an employee assistance professional, follow-through may be more likely. Ask the employee if you can help in any way with what's causing these problems.

Although it can be difficult to intervene, it is possible. Review again the tips provided in the previous Chapter under "Preparing for a Discussion about the Issue" (Section 9.1). Additionally, take note of the following suggestions:

- **Be aware of your communication style, including non-verbal behaviour and gestures.** For example, pointing or shaking your finger at an employee is generally intimidating. You're more likely to achieve a positive outcome if the employee views you as receptive and empathetic, rather than giving a scolding or being a critical parent. Maintain eye contact, speak in a moderate or soft tone, and demonstrate caring. Remember the old saying, *"People don't care what you know until they know that you care"*.

- **Praise the employee** when you see signs of progress. This kind of positive reinforcement is important for any staff member and especially for the depressive.

- **Don't ignore future behaviour problems**. This only serves to reinforce the problem behaviour.

"I knew I wasn't myself and hadn't been for some months, except I didn't know that it showed. The breakup with my boyfriend had been difficult. It hit me hard. On top of that my best friend was killed in a car crash. Both were unexpected, and the funeral for my girlfriend was awful and emotionally draining. I miss her so much... and I'll always remember her. It just seemed that all the people close to me were leaving or going away.

I found it difficult to concentrate at work and I really felt so de-motivated. Little things would set me off and I'd cry. At work, I'd hurry off to the toilets and try to compose myself before coming back to my desk. I also didn't want to socialise much and would make up excuses for not going to after-work drinks on Friday nights.

I took off a few days here and there from work and just stayed in bed most of the day. I felt so tired and fatigued. Some days I found it difficult to get out of my own way.

A couple of my girlfriends tried to cheer me up and take me out for a meal or to the movies. I really didn't know what was wrong with me. I just thought that I'd had a bit of a hard time lately and I'd get over it.

My boss was really well-liked by everyone and he asked me to go and have a coffee with him at a coffee shop around the corner from the office. He said that he'd noticed that I hadn't been myself lately and that he also noticed that my work seemed to be slipping. He knew about my boyfriend leaving and my girlfriend dying. He said that he felt that I might be depressed, and wondered if I should maybe see a psychologist. He said that having depression was not a life sentence, and that with help I should recover and be back to my old self. I hadn't thought I was depressed, but I thought a lot of my boss and I took his advice. I'm glad I did."

10.2 Medication Non-compliance

It's estimated that medication non-compliance is to blame for half of all unsuccessful treatments for depression. Treatment can fail because patients simply stop taking their medication too soon. Why would patients discontinue taking drugs that may improve the quality of their lives, and perhaps even save their lives? The most common reasons are:

- Unacceptable side effects, such as weight gain or sexual dysfunction
- The person feels better in the short-term and decides they are cured and no longer need medication
- The person believes their symptoms are controllable without medication
- Fear of addiction
- Lack of education about the biological components of depression
- Discrepancies between the doctor's instructions and what the patient remembers being told
- Failure to respond to medication and/or dosage
- Difficulty maintaining the dosage schedule due to inconvenience or neglect
- A chronic co-morbid condition, such as substance abuse, which causes the person to forget or to be out of control
- Cost of prescriptions

In the USA for example, medication compliance can be enhanced by ensuring that your organisation's ongoing investment in drug benefits is well spent by making medications more affordable through good drug insurance benefits, where applicable. In countries like Australia though, compliance can be assisted by managers and HR managers working with front-line doctors, psychologists, psychiatrists, and pharmacists to develop compliance programs that motivate individuals to take ownership of their treatment.

It's important to ensure that patients are educated about the benefits of compliance and the dangers of non-compliance. Doctors must take the time to thoroughly assess their patients to ensure an accurate diagnosis, educate them about their illness, tell them exactly what to expect, and monitor their progress. They should prepare them for the side effects of medications and explain what improvement will feel like and how long it will take.

Doctors must also maintain oversight to ensure that patients keep taking their medication. Duke University Medical Center studies show that up to 44% of patients starting drug therapy discontinue the drug within three months, and 28% of patients discontinue their anti-depressants within one month, often before the drug has even had a chance to work.[1]

A pharmacy care program can also play a role in enhancing medication compliance. Such a program might include personalised medication education, specially packaged medications (such as blister packs) that help patients remember to take their meds in appropriate dosages, and periodic follow-up by pharmacists. During prescription fulfillment, patients can be educated on the indications, strengths, adverse effects and usage instructions.[2]

Managers can also influence compliance. Of course, managers are not expected to be psychiatrists or counsellors, but simply maintaining regular contact with the employee and monitoring how they are doing using the GRO-DOH model allows managers to pick up on medication non-compliance issues.

Ask the employee, "Are you still taking your medication?" If the answer is "Yes", praise them for staying on their program and encourage them for doing the right thing. If the answer is "No", then ask, "Why not? What's happened?"

If their doctor has recommended that they discontinue their medication, then the task of the manager is simply to monitor the mood, behaviour, and performance of the employee. Continue to have GRO-DOH conversations until you, as the manager, can see consistent and sustained performance from your employee.

If the employee has discontinued the medication themselves ("I really don't like taking drugs of any kind"), then suggest that this may not be a good idea, and that they ought to discuss it with their doctor. It's important not to be heavy-handed or disciplinary in any way. That's not your job, after all; you're not the treating professional. However, continue to monitor their general mood, behaviour and performance, and continue to have the GRO-DOH conversations on a regular basis, such as every two weeks.

Employers can enhance medication compliance by providing a supportive recovery environment in the workplace, which we'll discuss in more detail in Chapter 11, "Working With A Depressed Co-worker".

10.3 Psychotherapy Non-compliance

Patients leave therapy for many reasons. They may start out with good intentions, but somehow motivation wanes. The most common reasons are:

- The stigma attached to psychotherapy
- Lack of education about the benefits of psychotherapy
- The patient feels better in the short-term and decides they're cured and no longer need psychotherapy
- The person believes their symptoms are controllable without psychotherapy
- Cost of psychotherapy
- Inconvenience, work and family scheduling conflicts, and feeling that it's too much of a bother
- Therapy hurts; the patient may not feel better immediately, and in fact, may feel worse in the short term

The best way to ensure a positive patient outcome is to diagnose and treat depressed patients correctly, and for a long enough period of time. Naturally, this is not the manager's job. We can only trust that the treating professional does their job well.

Immediate cure only happens in the movies. Continued patient education is perhaps the simplest, safest way to alleviate confusion and ensure that patients have realistic expectations of therapy. Patient-doctor misunderstandings are not uncommon, especially when the patient has a disorder that can impair cognition, such as clinical depression, and certainly bipolar disorder. Needless to say, therapists must develop good rapport with their patients, and the patient-therapist relationship must be grounded in trust.

In situations in which employers provide insurance coverage, they can enhance compliance by choosing a plan which covers the cost of therapy. Further, the HR department can organise a database and network of competent psychologists and psychiatrists. Failing that, certain bodies such as the local chamber of commerce or the local management body (e.g., Institute of Managers and Leaders) may have a referral network on their books. Finally, flexible scheduling or rostering by the manager that accommodates time off for therapy sessions is helpful.

10.4 Compliance Reduces Risks for Employers

Enhancing compliance interventions can help employers reduce exposure to risk. For example, if you have evidence that a depressed employee may become violent in the workplace, certainly you must – and are legally allowed to – remove the employee. No organisation is required to tolerate a violent employee, disabled or not.

Employers can face the risk of lawsuits if they don't properly handle depressed employees whom the courts would deem disabled. What are employers required to do to accommodate a depressed employee?

In general, laws such as the Americans with Disabilities Act, and the Human Rights Legislation Amendment Bill in Australia require employers to accommodate a depressed employee's physical or workplace needs if:

- the employee requests the accommodation
- the employee is taking steps to be treated successfully
- the requested accommodation is reasonable, i.e. not extremely costly or complicated

An example of a reasonable request might be for example, a depressed employee who is having trouble concentrating requests that a visual barrier, such as a room divider, be added to the office space.

A court case was reported involving a teacher who was diagnosed with depression, and his employer, who in this case was a Department of Education. The teacher considered that his requests for assistance were not being heard, and he therefore "dismissed" himself and did not return to work.

Judgment in the above matter was delivered on May 21, 2008. The judge found in favor of the plaintiff (the teacher) and, largely accepting his evidence, found that the defendant (the Department of Education) had breached its duty by failing to properly follow up on complaints made by the plaintiff about his workloads, and failing to deal with a grievance lodged by the plaintiff about workplace issues. As a result of the defendant's breach of mutual trust and confidence, as implied in the employment contract, the judge held that the plaintiff was entitled to treat the contract as repudiated, and therefore to terminate the contract and to constructively dismiss himself.

The plaintiff was initially awarded damages comprising past and future loss of earnings and loss of superannuation entitlements of $369,100, which was later amended to an amount of $392,000 (the judge had made an error in calculating interest).

Many employers have found that taking a few crucial steps to facilitate treatment and create a supportive work environment isn't all that costly or complicated, and that by encouraging employees to seek accommodations, they also encourage treatment, which boosts productivity, reduces absenteeism, and ultimately enhances the company's bottom line.

Again, using the GRO-DOH model means that either when you're discussing the "Options", or at the end when you're discussing the "Homework", you can ask what might support the employee or assist them at work as they recover and become stronger.

10.5 What Behaviour Constitutes Non-compliance?

What behaviour constitutes non-compliance on the job, and what are ways to address this issue? Let me describe such a scenario.

In a nutshell, the employee is recruited to do a job or task. As the manager, if you observe that they are not performing in some way (e.g., missed deadlines, absences from work, turning up late for work, withdrawing and not socialising, and so on), it is important that you document the situation and any discussion you have with the employee about it. Keep notes; this is important. If the poor performance continues, you should plan a discussion using the GRO-DOH guidelines (see Chapter 9).

If the staff member does not follow through on what was agreed to in the GRO-DOH discussion, and the poor behaviour continues, you should immediately have a further GRO-DOH conversation. If the employee agrees to take action (e.g., to seek professional help), but the behaviour continues, you will need to performance manage them.

Inform your HR department (if applicable) that you are going to initiate the performance management process because the individual has demonstrated that they are unwilling to do anything about their behaviour, and that to allow it to continue will only create poor morale in the team and impact productivity (and possibly safety). There really is no other alternative. "You can take a horse to water, but you can't make it drink", as the saying goes. You have given the employee every opportunity to get help and change their behaviour, but they have not complied. You are therefore compelled to take more formal action by way of performance management. If this strategy does not prove fruitful, then ultimately, they will need to leave the company. Sad but true.

"Things in my life were going okay in that I had just gotten my Masters and was starting a new job in a week. My family was really proud of me, but inside, I was feeling really terrible.

At first, I was feeling sad all the time, even though I had no reason to be. Then at times I would get angry and little things would set me off. I started to have fights with friends and family and was more abusive, for instance, to other motorists out on the road. I felt bad about myself and felt that I wasn't good enough for anyone. At times, it would get so bad that I'd wish that I could go to bed and not wake up.

My older brother, whom I looked up to and admired, took me out for a coffee and told me straight that I wasn't acting my usual self, and that everyone in the family had noticed a change in me. He said he thought that I was depressed and that I should go to our local doctor and check it out. I don't like doctors, never have, and so I told him, "No way, you've got to be joking!"

After a month on the job, I started to have problems at work. Sometimes, I just wouldn't show up because I couldn't sleep the night before and I just couldn't get out of bed. I also started to feel tired and worn out. My boss had a few words in my ear about punctuality and responsibility, but I kept not showing up. I got fired, and then I thought that maybe my brother was right and that I'd better get help.

I saw my general practitioner at the health clinic and he said that he thought that I had a common illness called depression, and that treatment could help. He referred me to a psychologist who attended at the same clinic, and I saw him for 'talking therapy' which helped me control my depression in my everyday life.

It's taken a while, but I'm starting to feel my old self again."

Chapter 10 Summary

Some employees deny that they have a problem. Some employees may refuse assistance. Others may accept assistance, but then abandon treatment before recovery can be achieved.

Others agree to get help, but don't follow through on either taking their medication or seeing their professional therapist regularly.

In such cases, refer to the GRO-DOH model discussed in Chapter 9, and persevere to try to make the employee accountable.

If the employee continues to not comply with the agreements that you made together, and continues with the poor behaviour, then the only other step is to initiate a formal performance management strategy. They stand to lose their job. Sad but true.

CHAPTER 11

Working With a Depressed Co-worker

Introduction

A depressed employee's performance may slowly deteriorate over months or even years, and the employee may not even be aware of it. Odds are good though, that co-workers are certainly aware of it.

Colleagues are usually more aware of what is happening than the boss or the depressed worker themselves. Sometimes a supportive co-worker can be the linchpin in motivating a depressed person to seek help, as well as an effective intervention liaison between management and the depressive person.

It's normal to feel uncertain about how to communicate with a co-worker who is depressed. Some co-workers are concerned that they may push their colleague over the edge. Some are fearful of interacting with someone with a mental disorder and would rather keep their distance. Others feel that there are other staff members who are better qualified to deal with a depressive than they are.

There are no definitive correct actions. But there are strategies that have a good chance of being helpful and can prevent the problem from escalating. Remember that the depressed person is a human being just like you and becoming depressed can happen to any one of us.

11.1 Basic Tools

There are three basic tools to use when initiating help.

The first is to **listen**.[1] When you discuss the issue, you'll be tempted to defend your viewpoint, to push back, to debate what the depressive says. Don't! There's no point in trying to *win* the conversation. Try to understand their perspective, paraphrase what they say, and repeat it back to them. Use statements such as, *"What you're saying is…"* or *"What I heard you say was…"*

Secondly, **ask questions**. *"How do you think you're really doing?" "Are you satisfied with your work at this time?"* Asking questions gets the co-worker thinking and obliges them to respond. When they respond, **listen**.

Thirdly, as will be discussed below, you need to **give feedback** to the depressed person. It is important to tell them what you observe and what you are aware of.

Often, the depressed person is in such a mental state that they lose touch with the reality of how they are acting. This is especially so if the decline has been gradual. We only really know ourselves in respect to those around us and how we relate to them. It is difficult to know ourselves in a vacuum. We all need feedback. As the saying goes, "Feedback is the breakfast of champions!"

11.2 How Can You Help the Depressed Co-worker?

11.2.1 Be An Ally, Not An Enemy

Your goal is to elicit cooperation from the co-worker, for the co-worker's own good and for the good of the company. Be patient. Denial and blaming others may be the individual's natural way of coping with an unpleasant reality. If the co-worker is angry or uncooperative, try to view their responses in the context of depression's ugly grip. It's important to try to build rapport and establish trust.

For example, reassure the employee with empathic statements such as:

"I know it must be scary [confusing, frustrating, debilitating]..."

"I know you may feel that your life is out of control [in a black hole, in a desperate place]..."

"I'm not trying to have a go at you, I'm on your side."

11.2.2 Reaching Out

Don't be afraid to reach out and ask someone how they're doing. Offering understanding and support can have a tremendous impact. Try to engage them, and include them in social activities.

Ask open-ended questions. Tell them you're concerned about their health, and depending on their response, suggest that they might be depressed.

11.2.3 Offering Feedback

As has already been said, feedback is the breakfast of champions. All your colleagues and co-workers need your feedback at various times. Naturally, there is a time and place to give feedback, and it ought to be done in a constructive, non-threatening way and away from public view.

For example, you might say:

"I've noticed that you just don't seem to be yourself lately, in that you're keeping to yourself and less likely to join in. What's happening for you?"

"I've been aware that you don't come to our happy hours or birthday lunches anymore. Is everything alright?"

"I've noticed that you seem more short and abrupt than you used to be, and I'm wondering what might be going on for you?"

11.2.4 Offering Help

Encourage them to make an appointment with their doctor, an employee assistance provider, psychologist or psychiatrist. Help them get more information about the symptoms, causes and treatment of depression. Follow up and ask how it turned out.

"My father founded the business twenty-three years ago and then mother, who is a lawyer, joined him to help run it. The business has done well.

I've been in the business now for three years as the General Manager, and in that time, growth and profit has been substantial. However, we are having trouble going forward and planning our business goals for the future because father, who is getting old now, I think is having trouble letting go.

I was really surprised at a family meeting that we had a month ago during which he broke down and cried, and said that there was no role for him any longer. It occurs to me now that the issues that we've been having in the last eighteen months or so are probably due to father feeling that he has no purpose any longer. I think he might actually be depressed.

I spoke to a psychologist for advice and we decided that it was Mother who has the best relationship with Father. She takes a 'softly, softly' approach, unlike me who tends to be direct and a bit blunt. We asked her to bring it up with Dad. It took about eight weeks or more before he agreed to see someone about it.

He is a proud man, but he did see the male psychologist who was older, was very experienced, and had grey hair, and I think that helped! Dad seems to be getting on better now, but if it hadn't been for Mum's approach, I'm not sure what we would have done."

11.3 What Support Is Not Helpful?

Because discussing depression with a co-worker can feel awkward, it is easy to say and do the wrong thing. But that's no reason not to try. However, it's **not** helpful to:

- Dismiss their mood swings, telling them, *"It's nothing"*. Don't trivialize their behaviour. It is something that needs to be acknowledged.

- Give well-intentioned advice that is largely gratuitous, for example, telling them that they just need to stay busy, or that they'll get over it.

- Encourage them to party and numb painful feelings with alcohol, drugs, or by having a good time. The depressed person needs to get in touch with themselves and their feelings, not try to discount them.

- Criticize, belittle or threaten to report their behaviour to a supervisor.

11.4 Communicating with a Supervisor

Sometimes it becomes necessary to discuss a troubled co-worker with the co-worker's supervisor. Reducing the costly headaches of low productivity and employee turnover are clear incentives for encouraging employees to feel comfortable about approaching a supervisor to discuss a depressed co-worker.

Employees must understand why it's important to help their organisation preserve its resources – including human capital – and to see themselves as participating in a partnership, rather than as tattling to the boss about a co-worker.

Reports to management should be about presenting the facts, rather than reporting problems from an emotional point of view. Ideally, the depressed co-worker's performance problems should be documented. The simple step of letting a supervisor intervene when performance is an issue may be all it takes to resolve the problem. This also keeps the communication at more of an objective level where you report the facts re job performance which then provides the boss or supervisor with an alert that all may not be well.

11.5 How Can Employers Provide Support?

11.5.1 Provide Support to At-risk Employees

Some employees are more vulnerable to mental health problems than others. Make sure they know that help through an EAP, community program or health clinic is available. An individual's psychological vulnerability can be enhanced by factors such as:

- Nearing retirement age
- Medical conditions that can trigger depression, such as a recent heart attack
- Alcohol or drug abuse
- A high-stress job or task — you likely know about stress hotspots within your organisation
- Pregnancy, or women who have recently given birth
- Recent bereavement or divorce
- Recent severe trauma

Developing and implementing workplace support strategies can help head off depression at the pass. Strategies can target specific workers or groups of workers.

This is usually not the manager's job, but the company may have these programs or strategies already in place, so it's important to remind the depressed person of their existence. Some examples might include:

- A support group for working mothers
- Support for employees nearing retirement to help ease the transition
- Counselling for employees who have experienced a traumatic event
- Counselling or coaching for employees who have high-stress jobs
- Counselling for employees who recently experienced bereavement or divorce
- Interventions for employees with hazardous drinking patterns
- Periodic depression screening events
- Social networks designed to support isolated workers

11.5.2 Designate Mentor Co-workers

Designating special mentor co-workers, or buddies, can help foster workplace resilience by providing additional support to depressed employees. In some cases, empathetic co-workers who are well-trained in how to support depressives, and well-informed about the organisation's policies, may achieve better results than the support offered by a supervisor, EAP or an outside professional.

The role of a mentor co-worker will include listening, educating, enhancing motivation, and offering advice that will help the depressed worker improve work performance and seek appropriate treatment. Mentor co-workers can also be effective liaisons between workers and management, if necessary.

One common way to select buddies is through a volunteering process in which expressions of interest are called for from employees, so that management can compile a list of appropriate mentors. Once a group of possible mentors has been gathered, the selection procedure is determined by factors such as the following:

- Is the person seen as empathic? Do they naturally have people coming to them with issues? Are they generally seen as a people-person?

- Do they have good listening skills? Mentors are not meant to be therapists, just supportive listeners.

- Are they good communicators who can liaise well between the depressed worker and management? Often the depressed person lacks the skills and capacity to be able to adequately communicate their issues. A mentor is ideally placed to act as a go-between, or at least to be present in meetings and discussions with the depressed person.

Chapter 11 Summary

An employee's performance may slowly deteriorate over months or even years, and the employee may not even be aware of it. Odds are good, though, that co-workers are aware of it. Colleagues are often more aware of what is happening than the boss or the depressed worker themselves.

Sometimes a supportive co-worker can be the linchpin in motivating a depressed person to seek help, as well as an effective intervention liaison between management and the depressive.

For the co-worker, there are certain do's and don'ts. Some workers are frightened to say or do anything in relation to the depressed worker for fear of making things worse, or because they don't want to get involved. Common sense will tell you, though, to reach out to someone to try to give a helping hand. This chapter suggests several ways of doing just that.

"Depression is not sobbing and crying and giving vent, it is plain and simple reduction of feeling...People who keep stiff upper lips find that it's damn hard to smile."

Judith Guest, 1936-
American novelist and screenwriter

CHAPTER 12

Trouble at the Top:
What To Do When Your Boss is Depressed

Introduction

Handling a depressed co-worker is one thing, but what do you do when you believe that your own supervisor or manager is suffering from depression? Who do you turn to for help in this instance?

12.1 The Boss is Depressed

The inherent boss-employee power imbalance often makes it difficult for employees to confront a depressed boss. Many fear reprimand or retaliation, particularly if they perceive their boss as difficult or hard to get along with.

Successfully managing a difficult boss is always a challenge, no matter what the situation. Managing a *depressed* difficult boss is an even greater challenge. Yet, empowering employees to do just that is a critical step in reducing overall stress in the workplace, and ultimately, lessening the grip of workplace depression.

Depressed employees often cite their bosses as a contributing cause of their own depression. Surveys show that up to half of all workers have shaky, if not downright miserable relationships with their supervisors. According to a Gallup poll, **a "bad relationship with the boss" is the number one reason for quitting a job**. Supervisor problems outpaced all other areas of worker dissatisfaction, including salary, work hours, and day-to-day duties.[1]

If many employees are leaving *supervisors*, not companies, effectively managing trouble at the top can clearly boost retention, not to mention productivity. Employees who work for happy and productive managers are more likely to be happy and productive themselves. The boss who is persistently negative, insecure, withdrawn, uncommunicative, irritable or critical – behaviours which you might expect to find in a depressed supervisor – drags the employee and the whole organisation down.

Emotions can be literally contagious. **Workers are susceptible to picking up the negative emotions that the boss spreads around.**

In *Resonant Leadership*, Richard E. Boyatzis and Annie McKee point out the two types of close relationships that seem to be particularly susceptible to emotional contagion: intimate partnerships and power relationships.[2] In romantic relationships for example, emotions are symbiotic. If one partner is feeling bad, the other suffers. One person's good mood can give the other a lift, too. But between boss and employee, emotion tends to flow in one direction – downhill. A supervisor's negativity pools with employees like stagnant water.

How workers feel about their managers affects their physical and psychological health. In fact, extensive research across many work sectors indicates that rapport with the boss largely predicts risk for depression and other psychiatric problems in the workplace. When it comes to overall well-being, a worker's relationship with their boss is nearly equal in importance to the relationship with their spouse. Even friendly co-workers, or a rewarding occupation, cannot compensate for a negative relationship with the boss.[1]

12.2 What's the Solution?

Empower employees. Easy to say, but not easy to do. It means creating an environment that precludes their feeling like victims of circumstances beyond their control.

Empower employees by educating them. Educate them about the symptoms, causes and treatments for depression. Education can take the form of a brief during an induction program or may be a dedicated training program of an hour or a half-day, with update sessions as part of more general company training.

Further, establish policies and procedures for handling the delicate matter of the depressed boss. Delegate this task to HR (or an outside, external HR consultant), and ensure that such policies are not just words on paper. Staff are quick to judge whether it is just more "stuff", or whether, instead, supervisors are people of their word who can be trusted.

Make sure that employees are aware of their options, and are encouraged to come forward with legitimate grievances. Make sure that the steps that staff need to take are clear and obvious. Don't make it complicated or protracted. The KISS principle reigns.

Do your best to handle the first case of a depressed boss effectively in order to instill confidence in the procedures that you have put in place. Follow the procedures laid down to the letter and give the employee who is reporting the situation adequate time and attention. **Remember, "The eyes of the world are upon you"**. Mess this up, and it doesn't matter how many policies or procedures you put in place, you won't get their trust again for years.

It may be necessary to protect the confidentiality of an employee who reports concerns about a supervisor. If employees fear reprimand or retaliation by their supervisors, they're unlikely to come forward with information that, handled in a timely and appropriate manner, could have facilitated an early – and more effective – intervention. When employees are given responsibility for managing their work relationships, they tend to be less anxious and more highly motivated. The result, ultimately, is a healthy, resilient workplace.

12.3 Employee Tips for Handling the Depressed Boss

12.3.1. Determine the Cause

Try to determine the cause of your supervisor's behaviour. Assuming your boss generally behaves in a fairly reasonable manner, and that their difficult behaviour seems to be a result of stress overload rather than character, chances are good that the behaviour can be modified. If your boss' behaviour is chronically hostile and abusive, regardless of the degree of stress at the worksite, the chances that the behaviour can change or alter are certainly less or minimal.

12.3.2. Examine Your Own Behaviour

Manage your own negative emotions regarding your boss' behaviour so that you do not engage in self-defeating behaviour. Don't resort to defiance, stonewalling or counter-attacking. Try to control your impulses to react emotionally or defensively. You may feel that your boss has been unjustifiably angry and bullying lately, and often criticises you unfairly. Try not to view the criticism as a personal attack. Try to separate your personal ego from your business persona.

Be careful to sort truth from fiction. Do you deserve some criticism too? Can you view this as an opportunity to improve your own performance as well? Viewing yourself through your boss' eyes will help you avoid misattributing their motives.

12.3.3. Communicate Effectively

Once you understand and have managed your own negative reactions, focus on communicating your issues and concerns, but frame them in a helpful, positive context. Your goal is to create an atmosphere that lends itself to problem resolution. Try to view your working relationship with your boss as a partnership, rather than viewing yourself as the victim of a power struggle.

Don't criticise. Discuss your concerns. There is a difference. Laying out your concerns in a non-adversarial way helps prevent further damage to the relationship. The odds of making the boss angry and provoking retribution will be significantly reduced if you can discuss problems in a reasonable, diplomatic, non-defensive manner.

Starting the conversation is always difficult. Schedule a time to see the boss in their office. You may or may not wish to leave the door open. If the boss is a yeller or a screamer, then it is wise to keep the door open. Otherwise, close the door. Some staff wait until they have their performance appraisal interview (which can occur every 6 months or perhaps annually) as a time to bring up the issue.

1. Begin with:

> "I'm hesitant about bringing up this issue because…[I don't want you to get it out of proportion; I don't want you to take it the wrong way; I don't want to cause offence; I really want you to see this in the right way]" (or words to that effect).

> It is important to start this way because it dispenses with small talk, and gets right to the issue. Plus, it squarely sets the tone for what is to follow.

2. Describe what you see and hear.

> "I've noticed lately that you have not been saying 'Good morning' to us when you arrive and have tended to shut yourself away in your office."

> "You don't seem to be giving us any leadership at present, and when you do delegate, you tend to do it in a gruff manner."

> "If I ask for clarification, you tend to get annoyed easily and raise your voice."

3. Describe the effect that it has on you and others.

"What this means is that we are generally worried about you since you're not your old self. Staff morale around here is not good, and a couple of people are talking about leaving. We really can't go on like this since it is starting to take its toll on me and the others."

4. Ask what you'd like to know.

"We wondered what was going on with you, and if there is anything that we can do to help?"

"What can we do to resolve this situation and restore positive morale around here?"

5. Listen to the boss' response.

Paraphrase and repeat back what the boss says to be sure there is consensus. Remember to hold onto your own emotions. This is not about you. It's about your boss. Just listen.

If the boss gets hostile, debates the issue, cries or withdraws, don't be put off. Hang in there. Use your reflective listening techniques and stay with the issue. Don't make this personal.

6. Push for an action.

By this time in the conversation, you may well be wishing that you'd never started it, or that somehow it might end! Alternatively, the conversation may be going well, and you are understanding each other.

Either way, there needs to be a resolution about what to do next. If you've gone to the trouble of gathering the courage to have this conversation, then don't drop the ball on the goal line. Something needs to happen. Will it be another meeting? Will the boss consider what you've said and get back to you?

12.3.4. Consult a Professional if Necessary

Still feel overwhelmed? If your boss has reacted badly to the conversation, or if you feel unable to manage your manager, you may want to consider seeking counsel from a trusted mentor or a human resources professional who can help you evaluate your options and also perhaps bring in objective mental health professionals, if necessary. Collaborating with a professional who has authority over the situation removes the responsibility from your shoulders of having to fix your boss, and helps you manage your own stress.

Chapter 12 Summary

Depressed bosses are not good news. Depressed employees often cite their bosses as a contributing cause of their own depression. Further, surveys show that a "bad relationship with the boss" is the number one reason for quitting a job.

If you see the signs and symptoms of depression in your boss, you should consult with the HR department or a trusted mentor who may be able to intervene.

If there is no such person to help, this chapter offers suggestions for that difficult conversation with your boss about their behaviour. Not always easy, but do-able.

"People don't leave bad companies. They leave bad leaders."

Betsy Allen-Manning,
American motivational speaker

CHAPTER 13

The Breakdown:
Managing a Personal Crisis in the Workplace

Introduction

Sometimes there's a straw that breaks the camel's back, and it can happen right in front of you – a co-worker or subordinate in crisis, crying uncontrollably, or perhaps staring off into the distance, detached, unable to perform the simplest job tasks or even think for themselves. Perhaps it is an outburst of anger or aggression towards someone or towards a group. Maybe it is property being destroyed. Whatever it is, it's a crisis.

13.1 Crisis Time

What do you do if a co-worker or colleague "loses it"? Certainly, the best route to crisis management is prevention. In other words, don't wait until a crisis strikes to put a strategy in place. A personal crisis can quickly become a business crisis.

With access to the appropriate depression management resources, employees are likely to be more resilient, better able to cope with stress, and less vulnerable to breaking down in the first place.

Having educated your employees about how to handle a co-worker breakdown can help restore workplace stability quickly and safely. Education can help employees understand the normal range of human responses to stress and how to recognise abnormal responses before they reach crisis point. Again, education can be via a brief training session, or through a more comprehensive mental health or well-being training program.

Ultimately, however, the organisation *must* have **a critical incident strategy** in place. The strategy should address not only a depressed person breaking down, but other crises as well, such as a fire, bomb scare, robbery, assault, heart attack or seizure.

13.2 Critical Incident Management Strategy

A Critical Incident Management Strategy is ultimately a risk management strategy. When responding to an employee mental health crisis in particular, it's important to:

1. Be proactive. Respond quickly and decisively, but humanely. Think long-term. Employees will remember how you handled the incident, even if they're not personally affected by it.

2. Move out of crisis mode quickly to mitigate overall workplace trauma and restore productivity quickly.

A **Critical Incident Management Strategy** might include tactics such as:

- The emergency response – **specific people in a unit, department or team need to be designated persons for when there is an emergency** (any emergency). People need to know who to go to. These people may be the health and safety representative for the area, the first aid person for the area, or the peer support person. This list of persons needs to be displayed clearly in the staff room, on the notice board, on the company's intranet site – and it needs to be updated regularly as people leave and are replaced. It also needs to be included in the induction process or in the orientation material handed out to new recruits. These designated people receive additional training in handling emergencies, and should be the ones who assist the depressed individual immediately, during and after the breakdown.

- **Coordination and feedback** about the incident with designated professionals, such as employee assistance providers is a key element of the process.

- **Debriefings**, conducted by experienced counsellors can provide everyone involved with an opportunity to discuss their feelings and thoughts in a controlled, rational manner. Information and sharing reduces uncertainty. Certainty reduces anxiety. A calm, trusting workforce buys you more time to resolve the problem.

- **Develop a crisis prevention plan**, which might include, for example, identifying hotspots for stress in your organisation and providing these specific workers with personalised assessment and counselling on an ongoing basis. This is often the role of employee assistance providers, who can usually determine the hotspots in an organisation and report back to the organisation on a regular basis.

13.3 Co-worker Response

In the heat of the moment when the depressed person breaks down, what should you do? Here are the necessary steps.

13.3.1 Accept Responsibility

If you witness the crisis (e.g., crying uncontrollably, talking nonsense and gibberish, staring into space and not acknowledging you, becoming angry or aggressive), you need to take over the situation and protect other staff members if necessary.

- Remove the traumatised staff member.

- Defuse the situation with the staff member, if necessary.

- Send someone to find the safety and health representative, first aid person, peer support worker, or other designated person. If none of them are available, keep following the steps below.

- Be aware of how other staff members in the vicinity are coping and designate someone to help them, if necessary.

13.3.2 Provide Assistance

- Find a quiet, private place to take the person to. Get them away from the commotion.

- Stop all incoming calls, have someone take messages, or take steps to eliminate interruptions.

- Get the person to take a walk with you, lie down, or drink something, or find some other appropriate way to distract them from their state of mind.

- Don't leave them alone.

13.3.3 Be Attentive and Listen

- Comfort them. Listen to them. Use eye contact.

- Pay attention and don't be distracted.

- Be reassuring and positive.

Follow these steps in order **to listen:**[1]

1. **Suspend judgment.** Don't jump to conclusions, apportion blame or be judgmental. Wait before responding. Let their message sink in. You don't have to say anything earth-shattering or give wise advice – just be there with them.

2. **Paraphrase.** If they want to talk, paraphrase what they say and repeat it back to them. This achieves four specific objectives:

   a. It conveys to the staff member that you are going to stay there with them, trying to understand what they are saying.

b. It helps to crystallize what the staff member has said in a more concise manner.

c. It helps the staff member continue to vent their feelings and move forward.

d. It provides a check for your own perceptions, and allows you to interpret what they're saying correctly.

3. **Ask questions.** Sometimes the staff member may want to tell you all about it. As they say, "A problem shared is a problem halved". Talking it out, seeking information and swapping experiences are natural ways to release tension and begin the process of resolving stress.

Your initial task is to stay out of the staff member's way and let them tell you how they see the situation. This is *not* a time for you to expound on your own life adventures and philosophy. Most useful in allowing the other to chat is giving them an open invitation to talk.

An **open invitation to talk** may be best understood when compared to a closed approach. For example:

Open:

> *"Tell me what happened?"*
> *"How did you feel about that?"*

Closed:

> *"Did he push you?"*
> *"Did you feel overwhelmed or anxious?"*

Open invitations to talk are extremely useful because:

- They help the staff member to elaborate on a point:

  "Could you tell me more about that?"
  "How did you feel when that happened?"
  "Can you explain that further?"

- They help elicit examples of specific behaviour so that you are better able to understand what the staff member is describing:

  "Can you give me a specific example?"
  "What do you mean you are shaky inside?"
  "What do you mean when you say that the customer was out of his mind?"

4. **Summarise.** Attempt to recapitulate, condense, and clarify the staff member's experience in your own words. A summary covers a relatively long time period, i.e. it puts together a number of the staff members' statements, an entire phase of the incident, or even an entire conversation.

For more information on Listening, go to www.drdarryl.com and under "Resources", download book called *"Listen Up Now"* or go directly to https://listenupnow.com.au for a hard copy or audio download.

13.3.4 Take Some Action

- Respond visibly, take notes about the crisis or make a call. Contact their doctor or treating mental health professional.

- Exceed expectations if at all possible:
    - Take them home.
    - Take them to their doctor.
    - Call their spouse or family.
    - Arrange for time off work.

13.3.5 Follow-up

If necessary, be prepared to visit the staff member at home or give them a call. Find out how they are doing, perhaps the next day, then in a few day's time, in a week, and in a month. Show you care. If you are the boss, then it is your job to care for your staff. If you are a colleague, appointed mentor-coworker, buddy, or peer support worker, for example, then it is also your job to care.

Following up is a great help when the depressed worker is ready to return to work, because the lines of communication are already open.

13.4 A Depressed Co-worker Becomes Violent in the Workplace

What do you do when a depressed person becomes aggressive or violent at work? According to the Bureau of Labor Statistics in the United States, there are over 1.5 million assaults in the workplace every year, more than 1000 of which are fatal. It is not being suggested that these cases are related to depressives, but only that violence certainly is a feature of the workplace (as it is in the general community).

If a depressed worker becomes violent towards others, or even towards goods and/or property, it is imperative to immediately make the area safe. If no one is prepared to stop the person being violent, either by talking them down or using physical restraint, then the police will need to be called.

If there is no designated person (e.g., a safety and health representative, first aid person, HR manager, or peer support worker) in the immediate area when the individual becomes violent, someone has to act. These are **the steps to follow**:

- Can you talk the person down?

  If yes, do so, and signal for someone to get help if possible. If no, then either protect yourself (e.g., retreat and lock the door), or advance and restrain the person physically. These choices are not made at a conscious level. They are made sub-consciously and quickly. You don't have time to think, you normally just act instinctively.

- Has the person calmed down?

  If yes, get help from the appropriate designated person (e.g., peer support worker, company nurse or doctor).

  If no, call the police and/or a mental health care crisis team. The former is called if damage to people or property is still occurring. The latter is called if the person is still "out of their mind", but not a danger to anyone.

- Once the crisis is over or the threat of violence reduced, take remedial action, take notes about the crisis, or make a call. Contact the employee's doctor or mental health care professional. See if you can assist further by:
  - Taking them home
  - Taking them to their doctor
  - Calling their spouse, partner or family
  - Arranging for time off work

- Once the depressed person has left the premises or the situation is again secure, check on the other workers. Determine whether you need to call a meeting **to debrief** and to release some of the emotion. **This would be the most common approach.** People need to share experiences, hear what others think and feel, and learn that they are not the only ones feeling that way. Let the group get things off their chests, get things more in perspective, and reduce their own stress levels.

- See if any workers need further attention or counselling. If so, refer them to the EAP for additional help.

- As before, follow up. This is not a time to isolate the worker. They may be feeling ashamed, guilty, or remorseful about their outburst or demonstration of aggression. Help build a bridge! Follow up that day or the next day or during the week.

- Continue to follow up. Keep in touch. This is imperative. The employee has to come back to work at some point, and you, as the manager, need to be assured that they are well enough and that their treating professional has approved the return. Organise a return-to-work program, which may be graduated (e.g., half-days for the first week, followed by alternate full days for week two and three, and so on), or with restricted or light duties for the first few weeks or months.

- You may want to call a meeting of all staff to prepare them for the employee's return. No doubt they will have questions about the illness and about their own safety. Such issues need to be discussed.

"I wanted to talk about it. Damn it! I wanted to scream. I wanted to yell. I wanted to shout about it. But all I could do was whisper, 'I'm fine'."

Author unknown

Chapter 13 Summary

It is advisable for the company to have a critical incident strategy in place for any emergency (e.g., fire, bomb threat, robbery, etc.) as well as for a situation in which a depressed person suddenly deteriorates (e.g., talks gibberish, stares into space, cries or sobs uncontrollably).

If you are the only one around when the depressed person breaks down, there are some standard steps to follow, including the following:

- Accept responsibility
- Give assistance
- Be attentive and listen
- Take some action
- Follow up

However, if the worker becomes violent towards others or property, and it's not possible to immediately talk them down, then physical restraint may need to be used as well as the police and/or a mental health care team being called.

Additional further critical steps to follow are outlined above as well as being aware that other staff in the near vicinity may need attention together with a group debriefing by a professional counsellor.

CHAPTER 14

The Consequences of Not Intervening

Introduction

It can be tempting for organisations to decide that workplace depression (and mental health issues generally) is too complex to tackle and to simply ignore it. *"People are difficult enough to manage without worrying about their personal issues such as depression. Besides, we have enough issues to contend with and none of us are mental health experts anyway."*

It's also easy to argue that there is too much that is going on and other issues need to take a higher priority. *"Besides, if the business isn't making a profit, then no-one has a job, including the depressed persons."*

But the costs and consequences of a non-intervention policy can be dramatic. When depressed employees don't receive timely managerial support and treatment, the outcome for employers can be negative and costly.

14.1 Untreated Depression Can Have a Devastating Impact

Consider the following scenarios:

- An employee returns to work following a breakdown, struggles to make the transition, suffers a relapse, and ends up on long-term disability.

- A once-productive employee's performance slips, and thinking that they are no longer up to the job, the manager demotes them.

- Unable to concentrate because of intrusive, negative thoughts, and too fearful to reveal the problem to management, an experienced employee quits without explanation.

- An employee acts inappropriately, for example, someone accuses them of spying or handling company funds fraudulently. Perhaps this behaviour is even out of character, yet no one recognises the signs of mental illness, and the person is fired.

These scenarios occur every day in some organisation somewhere. With proper managerial intervention, each of these negative outcomes could be transformed into a positive outcome.

Depression is a destabiliser, certainly for the depressive, but for the depressive's co-workers as well not to mention management. And depression is, famously, a morale destroyer. Consider, for example, these typical depressive behaviour patterns and their impact on morale:

- The employee who's not carrying their weight

- The angry, defiant employee
- The withdrawn, unsociable, "wet blanket" employee
- The sad sack, always melancholy and pessimistic
- The employee who commits suicide

"I thought things in my life were going all right, well, at least as well as could be expected, but inside, I was feeling terrible.

At first, I was feeling sad all the time, even though I really had no reason to really feel down. Then the sadness turned into anger and I started having fights with my family and really started to yell at the kids. I felt bad about myself, like I wasn't up to much. It got so bad that I wished I would go to bed and never wake up.

At work, my problems started to get worse too. I knew I wasn't across my job and I was late for work a number of times because I was just so tired and slept in. I missed a few important deadlines too. People at work really started to annoy me as well, and particularly one colleague. We had a stand-up argument over work roles and the boss called us into his office. He said our bickering and coolness to each other had affected morale in the office and he was arranging for us to go to mediation together. I was kind of shocked.

We went through mediation okay and kind of called a truce, but the professional pulled me aside afterwards and said he thought that I might be clinically depressed. This really caught me by surprise, but he said that it was a common illness and that treatment could help and he suggested seeing an EAP counsellor.

I started to see the counsellor each week for "talk" therapy and he also told me to see my general practitioner who put me on some medication. It seems to be working in that my depression isn't as bad now. It's taken some time, but I'm starting to feel a bit better. I think too that my work is improving in that the boss said at my last performance appraisal session that he felt things were settling down and were generally going okay now."

14.2 Why Do Some Employers Resist Establishing Intervention Programs?

Most employers are not sophisticated when it comes to mental health care issues. It's not what they are trained to do or watch out for. Toyota and Ford spend their time concentrating on cars, McDonald's and Hungry Jacks mostly on hamburgers. Corporations that are savvy about mental health care are the exception and not the rule.

Given the high toll that depression takes on the workplace, why don't all employers offer depression management and support programs? The reasons vary, but unfortunately, many of those reasons are based on myths. Let's debunk the most common myths.

MYTH: Workplace depression management programs cost too much and negatively impact profitability.

REALITY: The truth is, *not* responding to mental health issues in the workplace is *more* expensive, and workplace depression programs are actually more likely to positively impact profitability. The costs of absenteeism, retraining workers, disability benefits, lost productivity, and deterioration of worker morale quickly mount. Employers who believe that depression management programs are too costly don't understand the relationship between productivity and employee mental health. Responding to mental health problems in the workplace improves productivity.

MYTH: Our organisation is too small.

REALITY: Sometimes employers with only a few employees believe it will never happen to them, and do not employ someone who has the expertise to respond to mental health issues or do not use an outside consultant. In truth, addressing employee mental health can be even more critical for small businesses, since there are fewer workers to pick up the slack for a depressed, unproductive employee. Small businesses must also take into account the legal ramifications of not accommodating mental health disabilities. For example, employers in Australia have certain legal obligations to fulfil.[1] Similarly, in the U.S., employers with fifteen or more employees may have certain legal obligations under Title I of the Americans with Disabilities Act.[2]

MYTH: We don't have the money or resources to implement a mental health program.

REALITY: Depression management programs don't have to be expensive. There are many low-cost and no-cost ways to support depressed employees and encourage them to seek treatment. One option is to begin with strategies that require few resources, such as a program which educates workers about mental health issues. Employers can even partner with mental health services in the community for the purposes of educating employees or referring employees with mental health problems for treatment. Many governments offer funding for mental health and occupational safety initiatives, particularly for small workplaces. Collective employer organisations can be effective partners, allowing member companies to share expertise and strategies.

MYTH: Workplace interventions are not effective.

REALITY: Some employers are simply unaware of the impact of workplace depression or are unwilling to make changes to accommodate it. Workplace studies and pilot projects can help employers test strategies, and they illustrate the benefits. Respected medical and HR leaders can be instrumental in swaying the opinions of the naysayers, both in board meetings and open forums.

MYTH: Employers should simply not employ depressed people because depression is caused by personal weaknesses, and people with mental health problems never recover.

REALITY: First, employers should be aware of legislation that may prevent them from terminating depressed employees or discriminating against new recruits with mental health disabilities. With proper treatment and support, depressed workers can recover and go on to be some of the most productive employees. Second, depression is not caused by personal weaknesses. As we have seen in earlier chapters, it can happen to anyone, even those who consider themselves to be somehow immune to it. Lastly, the evidence is clear; with appropriate treatment, depressives do recover.

MYTH: Employees will not take advantage of mental health support opportunities if we offer them.

REALITY: When employees are educated about the benefits of treatment, provided with adequate support programs, and assisted in overcoming the stigma associated with mental illness, they're more likely to willingly participate in support programs.

Even before we headed into a world economic breakdown in 2008 and then into covid-19 in 2020, the trends and statistics indicated that depression was becoming a global problem anyway, and that by 2020, it was going to become the second most important cause of disability worldwide regardless. It is not too presumptuous therefore, to suggest that, given unprecedented declines in international financial markets and impending national recessions, plus significant international conflicts, along with major upheaval to life due to covid-19 measures having been implemented, that depression may well become the number one disability worldwide.

Furthermore, as we have seen, 70% of depressives are in the workforce. Hence, organisations and companies need to have in hand both rehabilitative and proactive programs to cope with this approaching (and current) epidemic.

Chapter 14 Summary

Companies that invest in their staff create a culture in which employees want to work for the organisation, productivity increases, and the organisation therefore prospers and is rewarded with profit. The myths working against depressives need to be de-bunked.

Investing in healthy human capital pays large dividends in the long run. The companies that invest in their workforces today will emerge tomorrow as the productivity leaders.

"Laugh at yourself and at life. Not in the spirit of derision or whining self-pity, but as a remedy, a miracle drug, that will ease your pain, cure your depression, and help you to put in perspective that seemingly terrible defeat and worry with laughter at your predicaments, thus freeing your mind to think clearly toward the solution that is certain to come. Never take yourself too seriously."

Og Mandino, 1923-1996
Inspirational author

REFERENCES

CHAPTER 1 REFERENCES

1. Hidaka, B.H. (2012). Depression as a disease of modernity: explanations for increasing prevalence. *J Affect Disorders* (November) 140 (3), 205-214. https://www.ncbi.nlm.nih.gov/pmc/articles/PMC3330161/

2. Pogosyan, M. (2017). How culture affects depression. *Psychology Today*, (December 6). https://www.psychologytoday.com/us/blog/between-cultures/201712/how-culture-affects-depression

3. World Health Organisation https://www.who.int/news-room/fact-sheets/detail/depression

4. Ng, C. W. M., How, C.H., & Ng, Y. P. (2017). Depression in primary care: assessing suicide risk, *Singapore Medical Journal*, 58 (2), 72-77. https://doi.org/10.11622/smedj.2017006

5. National Institute of Mental Health (USA). https://www.nimh.nih.gov/health/statistics/major-depression

6. National Institute of Mental Health. https://www.nimh.nih.gov/health/statistics/suicide

7. Ozama, H. (2009, January 10). One man's lonely cliff crusade saves 167 lost souls. *The Advertiser*.

8. Wang, S., Wright, R., & Wakatsuki, Y. (2020). https://edition.cnn.com/2020/11/28/asia/japan-suicide-women-covid-dst-intl-hnk/index.html

9. Hajkowicz, S. (2021). Mega Moves, *Company Director*, 37(6), 54-59.

10. Patten, S.B., Wang, J.L., Williams, J.V.A., Currie, S., Beck, C.A., Maxwell, C.J. & El-Guebaly, N. (2006). Descriptive epidemiology of major depression in Canada, *Canadian Journal of Psychiatry*, 51 (2), 84-90. doi: 10.1177/070674370605100204.

11. World Population Review. https://worldpopulationreview.com/country-rankings/depression-rates-by-country

12. Ludden, D. (2017). East-West Cultural Differences in Depression: Strategies for Coping with Negative Moods, *Psychology Today*, (November 20). https://www.psychologytoday.com/us/blog/talking-apes/201711/east-west-cultural-differences-in-depression

13. Creighton, A. (2021, September 28). Why comparing Covid-19 to the Spanish Flu is absurd. *The Australian.* https://www.theaustralian.com.au/commentary/its-making-history-but-not-in-a-good-way/news-story/4266d321e80eea03bc466c5f5e48db34

14. Mac Ghlionn, J. (2022, February, 5). Elon Musk is Right: The road to tyranny is paved with fear. *The Epoch Times.* https://www.theepochtimes.com/elon-musk-is-right-the-road-to-tyranny-is-paved-with-fear_4249364.html?utm_source=open&utm_medium=search

15. Mercola, J. & Cummins, R .(2021) *The Truth about Covid-19: Exposing the Great Reset, Lockdowns, Vaccine Passports and the New Normal.* London: Chelsea Green Publishing

16. Desmet, M. (2022). *The Psychology of Totalitarianism.* London: Chelsea Green Publishing

17. Hamilton, C. (2021, May 27) Where did COVID come from? The case for a leak of a virus engineered in a Wuhan lab, *Sydney Morning Herald.*

18. Grim, R (2023, June 17). Documents link potential covid patient zero to US-funded research in Wuhan. *The Intercept.*
https://www.theaustralian.com.au/commentary/its-making-history-but-not-in-a-good-way/news-story/4266d321e80eea03bc466c5f5e48db34

19. Geraghty, J. (2023, June 15). The truth about Covid's origin is coming out. *National Review.*
https://www.nationalreview.com/the-morning-jolt/the-truth-about-covids-origin-is-coming-out/

20. Lei Ravelo, J., & Jerving, S. COVID-19 in 2020 – a timeline of the coronavirus outbreak.
https://www.devex.com/news/covid-19-in-2020-a-timeline-of-the-coronavirus-outbreak-99634

21. World Health Organisation. https://covid19.who.int/

22. Labour Market Impacts. Retrieved from https://ilostat.ilo.org/topics/covid-19/

23. McKinsey Global Insititute (2020, April). COVID-19 and jobs: Monitoring the US Impact on People and Places.
https://www.mckinsey.com/industries/public-and-social-sector/our-insights/covid-19-and-jobs-monitoring-the-us-impact-on-people-and-places

24. Federal Reserve Bank of St Louis. (2020, October). How has the CCOVID-19 Pandemic Affected the US Labor Market? https://www.stlouisfed.org/open-vault/2020/october/how-covid19-pandemic-has-affected-labor-market

25. Congressional Research Serivce (August, 2021). Unemployment Rates During the COVID-19 Pandemic. https://sgp.fas.org/crs/misc/R46554.pdf

26. Parliament of Australia. (2020, October) COVID-19: Labour market impacts on key demographic groups, industries and regions

https://www.aph.gov.au/About_Parliament/Parliamentary
_Departments/Parliamentary_Library/pubs/rp/rp2021/CO
VID-19-Stat_Snapshot

27. National Skills Commission.
    https://www.nationalskillscommission.gov.au/reports/sha
    pe-australias-post-covid-19-workforce/part-1-labour-
    market-update/11-impact-covid-19-australian-labour-
    market

28. King, B. (2021, May 18). Unemployment rate: How many
    people are out of work? *BBC News*.
    https://www.bbc.com/news/business-52660591

29. Cross, D. (2022, January).
    https://www.linkedin.com/pulse/what-most-us-didnt-see-
    coming-deeper-levels-covid-19-darryl-
    cross/?trackingId=HKaipKEvQzCgTuEv79QCGA%3D%3
    D

30. OECD Policy Responses to Coronavirus (COVID-19).
    (2021). Tackling the mental health impact of the COVID-
    19 crisis: An integrated, whole-of-society response.
    https://www.oecd.org/coronavirus/policy-
    responses/tackling-the-mental-health-impact-of-the-
    covid-19-crisis-an-integrated-whole-of-society-response-
    0ccafa0b/

31. Santomauro, D.F, Herrera, A.M.M., Shadid, J, et al.
    (2021). Global prevalence and burden of depressive and
    anxiety disorders in 204 countries and territories in 2020
    due to the COVID-19 pandemic. *The Lancet*, 398
    (10312), 1700-1712
    https://www.thelancet.com/journals/lancet/article/PIIS014
    0-6736(21)02143-7/fulltext#%20

32. IHME (2021). New Global Burden of Disease analyses
    show depression and anxiety among the top causes of
    health loss worldwide, and a significant increase due to
    the COVID-10 pandemic.
    https://www.healthdata.org/acting-data/new-ihme-

analyses-show-depression-and-anxiety-among-top-causes-health-burden-worldwide

33. Panchal, N., Kamal, R., Cox, C., & Garfield, R. (2021, February). The implications of Covid-19 for mental health and substance use. https://www.kff.org/coronavirus-covid-19/issue-brief/the-implications-of-covid-19-for-mental-health-and-substance-use/

34. Czeisler, M.E., Lane, R.I., Petrosky, E., & Wiley, JF. (2020). Mental Health, Substance Use, and Suicidal Ideation During the COVID-19 Pandemic – United States, June 24-30, 2020 Weekly, August 14. https://www.cdc.gov/mmwr/volumes/69/wr/mm6932a1.htm

35. Abbott, A. (2021, February 3). COVID's mental health toll: How scientists are tracking a surge in depression. *Nature.* https://www.nature.com/articles/d41586-021-00175-z

36. Morganne, C. (2020, October 10) Canadians Reporting Higher Levels of Anxiety, Depression amid the Pandemic, *Global News Canada.* https://globalnewsca/news/7391217/world-mental-health-day-canada/

37. Cross, D (2021, February). The Pandemic Tail: It's called exhaustion. https://www.linkedin.com/pulse/pandemic-tail-its-called-exhaustion-darryl-cross/

38. DeWolfe, D.J. (2000). *Training manual for mental health and human service workers in major disasters* (2nd ed., HHS Publication No. ADM 90-538) Rockville, MD:US Deptment of Health and Human Services, Substance Abuse and Mental Health Services Administration, Center for Mental Health Services.

39. Peterson, C., Maier, S.F. & Seligman M.E.P. (1993). *Learned Helplessness: A Theory for the Age of Personal Control.* Oxford University Press

40. Mental Health Statistics: mental health at work. https://www.mentalhealth.org.uk/statistics/mental-health-statistics-mental-health-work

41. Goldberg, R.J., & Steury, S. (2001). Depression in the workplace: Costs and barriers to treatment, *Psychiatric Services, 52*,1639-1643.

42. Canadian Mental Health Association (2016, February28). https://cmha.ca/brochure/mental-illnesses-in-the-workplace/

43. Gurchiek, K. (2019, November 7). The paralysis of depression in the workplace. SHRM. https://www.shrm.org/hr-today/news/hr-news/pages/the-paralysis-of-depression-in-the-workplace.aspx

44. Gillard, J (2019, September 19). Australia loses eight million working days a year due to mental health issues. SBS News. https://www.sbs.com.au/news/mental-illness/australia-loses-eight-million-working-days-a-year-due-to-mental-health-issues

45. Mental health in the workplace. Mental Health Foundation. (2020, September 24). https://www.mentalhealth.org.uk/our-work/mental-health-workplace

46. CAMH: Workplace Mental Health (2020, January 6) https://www.camh.ca/-/media/files/workplace-mental-health/workplacementalhealth-a-review-and-recommendations-pdf.pdf?la=en&hash=5B04D442283C004D0FF4A05E366 2F39022268149

47. Mental Health Alliance. https://www.mhanational.org/depression-workplace

48. Lim, K-P., Jacobs, P., Ohinmaa, A., Schopflocher, D., & Dewa, CS (2008). A new population-based measure of

the economic burden of mental illness in Canada, *Chronic Diseases Canada*, 28(3), 92-98

49. Miller, D.M., Lipsedge, M., & Litchfield, P. (Editors). (2002). *Work and mental health, An employer's guide.* London: The Royal College of Psychiatrists.

50. Minor, M. (2021, January 20). Mental health in the workplace: The high cost of depression. https://www.forbes.com/sites/mariaminor/2021/01/20/mental-health-in-the-workplace-the-high-cost-of-depression/?sh=436ce8936666

51. Lednar, W.M. (2003). Mental health support needs: The employer's perspective in optimizing clinical and economic outcomes. *Managed Care Magazine*, 12 (Supplement) (7).

52. Goldberg, R.J., & Steury, S. (2001). Depression in the workplace: Costs and barriers to treatment, *Psychiatric Services, 52,*1639-1643.

53. von Heymann. C. (2008). C. Hard Dollars of Depression, *Benefits Canada*, Feb. 2008, 65.

54. Henry, J.A., & Rivas, C.A. (1997). Constraints on anti-depressant prescribing and principles of cost-effective antidepressant use. Part 1: depression and its treatment. *Pharmacoeconomics, 11,* 419-443.

55. Cross, M. (2006). Employers take lead in fighting depression. *Depression in the workplace* (suppl Managed Care Mag), 1, 13-20.

56. Kessler, R.C., Barber, C., & Birnbaum, H.G. (1999). Depression in the workplace: effects on short-term disability. *Health Affairs, 18,* 163-171

57. Sipkoff, M. (2006). Depression is prevalent and pernicious, costing employers billions each year the workplace. *Managed Care Magazine,* 1 (Supplement; Spring), 4-12.

58. Gabriel, P., & Liimatainen, M-R. (2000). Mental Health in the Workplace, Cornell University. http://digitalcommons.ilr.cornell.edu/gladnetcollect/223

CHAPTER 2 REFERENCES

1. Cross, D (2021, February). The Pandemic Tail: It's called exhaustion. https://www.linkedin.com/pulse/pandemic-tail-its-called-exhaustion-darryl-cross/

2. Olfson, M., Marcus, S.C., & Druss, B. (2002). National trends in the outpatient treatment of depression. *Journal of American Medical Association, 287*, 203-209.

3. American Psychological Association (APA)(2004, 2006). "Workplace Survey"

4. The Great Resignation: what it is and how can employers avoid it. (2021). https://www.consultancy.com.au/news/4439/the-great-resignation-what-is-it-and-how-can-employers-avoid-it

5. Catalano, C. (2007, April 24). Depression hits lawyers, *The Age*

6. The Top 10 Jobs with the Highest Rates of Depression. (2020). https://gatewaytms.com/the-top-10-jobs-with-the-highest-rates-of-depression

7. Monash University report identifies occupations with greater risk of suicide. (2020). https://www.monash.edu/medicine/news/latest/2020-articles/monash-university-report-identifies-occupations-with-greater-risk-of-suicide#:~:text=Nursing%20and%20Midwifery%3A%20Suicide%20risk,than%20those%20in%20other%20occupations

8. Hassed, C. (2006). *Mind-Body Medicine: Science, Practice and Philosophy,* Lecture notes, Dept of General Practice, Monash University, October 2006.

9. Chantiri, E. (2009). Dying for a holiday. *Business Review Weekly*, 21-27 May, 13.

10. Martin, S. (2008). Money is the top stressor for Americans. *Monitor on Psychology, 39* (11), 28-29.

11. Moss, J (2021). *The Burnout Epidemic: The rise of chronic stress and how we can fix it.* Boston, Massachusetts: Harvard Business Review Press.

12. Hazard factsheet 78. http://www.hazards.org/getalife

13. Goh, J., Pfeffer, J., & Zenits, A. (2016). The Relationship between Workplace Stressors and Mortality and Health Costs in the United States. *Management Science, 62* (2), iv-vii

14. Three our of Five Employees are Highly Stressed, According to ComPsych Survey (2017). https://www.compsych.com/press-room/press-article?nodeId=37b20f13-6b88-400e-9852-0f1028bd1ec1

15. American Psychological Association Survey Shows Money Stress Weighing on Americans' Health Nationwide. (2015). https://www.apa.org/news/press/releases/2015/02/money-stress

16. Dahlgren, A., Kecklund, G., & Akerstedt, T. (2005). Different Levels of Work-Related Stress and the Effects on Sleep, Fatigue and Cortisol. *Scandinavian Journal of Environmental Health, 31* (4), 277-285.

17. Ross, J. (2015). Only the Over-worked Die Young. *Harvard Health Blog.* https://www.health.harvard.edu/blog/only-the-overworked-die-young-201512148815

18. DeFilippis, E., Immink, S.M., Singell, M., Polzer, J.T., & Sadum, R (2020). Collaborating During Coronavirus: The Impact of COVID-19 on the Nature of Work. https://www.nber.org/papers/w27612

19. Davis, M.F., & Green, J. (2020). Three Hours Longer, the Pandemic Workday has Obliterated Work-life Balance. https://www.bloombergquint.com/coronavirus-outbreak/working-from-home-in-covid-era-means-three-more-hours-on-the-job

20. Pink, D.H. (2011). *Drive: The Surprising Truth About What Motivates us*. Canongate Paperback

21. Peterson, C., Maier, S.F. & Seligman M.E.P. (1993). *Learned Helplessness: A Theory for the Age of Personal Control.* Oxford University Press

22. Wagner, R. & Harter, J.K. (2006). *The 12 elements of Great Managing*. New York: Gallup Press

23. Workplace Bullying Institute (2007). *2007 WBI-Zogby U.S. Workplace Survey*. http://bullyinginstitute.org/zogby2007/wbizogby2007.html

24. Miller, D.M., Lipsedge, M., Litchfield, P. (Editors). (2002). *Work and mental health, An employer's guide*. London: The Royal College of Psychiatrists.

25. Leymann, H. (1996). *Mobbing and victimization at work: A Special Issue of the European Journal,* Psychology Press (Imprint of Taylor & Francis Group).

26. Kelleher, D. (2013). Survey: 81% of US Employees Check their Work Mail outside Work Hours. https://techtalk.gfi.com/survey-81-of-u-s-employees-check-their-work-mail-outside-work-hours/

27. Price, M (2009). Should clients disclose their mental illness? *Monitor on Psychology, 40*(1), 10.

28. Gabriel, P. & Liimatainen, M. (2000). *Mental health in the workplace: Introduction, executive summaries.* http://digitalcommons.ilr.cornell.edu/gladnetcollect/223

29. IBIS World. (2022). *Employee Assistance Program Services in Australia; Market Research Report* (May 9). https://www.ibisworld.com/au/industry/employee-assistance-program-services/5439/

CHAPTER 3 REFERENCES

1. American Psychiatric Association (2013). *Diagnostic and statistical manual of mental disorders, Fifth edition text revision (DSM-V-TR).* Arlington, Virginia.

2. Beaton Consulting. (2007). http://www.beaton.com.au/pdfs/BC_ProfessionsSurvey.pdf

3. Parker, G (2004). Dealing with Depression. Crows Nest, NSW: Allen & Unwin.

4. Manicavasagar, V. (2003). *New Perspectives in the Diagnosis and Treatment of Mood Disorders.* Randwick, NSW: Black Dog Institute.

5. Compton, M.T., & Kotwicki, R.J. (2007). *Responding to Individuals with Mental Illness*, Boston: Jones & Bartlett, 2007.

6. Treatment Protocol Project (2004). *Management of Mental Disorders (Fourth edition).* Sydney: World Health Organization.

7. Jamison, K.R. (1995). *An Unquiet Mind.* New York: Alfred A. Knopf.

CHAPTER 4 REFERENCES

1. American Psychiatric Association (2013). *Diagnostic and Statistical Manual of Mental Disorders,* Fifth Edition Text Revision (DSM-V-TR). Arlington, Virginia.

2. Patten, S., & Juby, H. (2008). A profile of clinical depression in Canada. *Research Synthesis Series, 1,* 1-23.

3. Compton, M.T. & Kotwicki, R.J. (2007). *Responding to Individuals With Mental Illnesses.* Sudbury, Massachusetts: Jones & Bartlett Publishers, Inc.

4. World Health Organization (WHO) (2002). Global Burden of Disease (GBD) 2002 Estimates," retrieved 21st January, 2009 from WHO website: http://www.who.int/healthinfo/globalburdendisease/estimates_regional_2002/en/

5. National Institute of Mental Health (NIMH), U.S. Department of Health and Human Services (1999). *Mental Health: A Report of the Surgeon General,* Rockville, MD: U.S. Department of Health and Human Services.

6. Office for National Statistics Psychiatric Morbidity, National Statistics (2001). http://www.statistics.gov.uk/

7. Andrews, G., Hall W., Teeson, M. & Henderson, S (1999). *The Mental Health of Australians.* Canberra: Mental Health Branch, Commonwealth Department of Health & Aged Care.

8. Patten, S.B., Wang, J., Beck, C., & Maxwell, C. (2005). Measurement issues related to the evaluation and monitoring of major depression prevalence in Canada. *Chronic Diseases in Canada, 26* (4), 100-106.

9. Hassed, C. (2006). *Mind-Body Medicine: Science, Practice and Philosophy.* Lecture notes, Dept of General Practice, Monash University, October.

10. Nolen-Hoeksema, S., Grayson, C., & Judith (1999). Explaining the Gender Difference in Depressive Symptoms. *Journal of Personality and Social Psychology*, *77*, (5).

11. Ozols, I., & McNair, B. (2007). *Mental Health: Creating a Mentally Healthy and Supportive Workplace*, Australia: mh@work.

CHAPTER 5 REFERENCES

1. Solomon, A. (2001). *Noonday Demon*. New York: Scribner, 2001.
2. Treatment Protocol Project (2004). *Management of mental disorders (Fourth edition)*. Sydney: World Health Organization.

3. American Psychiatric Association (2013). *Diagnostic and statistical manual of mental disorders, fourth edition text revision (DSM-V-TR)*. Arlington, Virginia.

4. Parker, G (2004). *Dealing with Depression*. Crows Nest, NSW: Allen & Unwin.

5. Fram, D.H. Editor. (2006). *Causes of Depression*. http://www.webmd.com/depression/guide/causes-depression

6. Department of Health and Human Services – U.S. (1999). *Mental Health: A Report of the Surgeon General*. Rockville, MD: U.S. Department of Health and Human Services, Substance Abuse and Mental Health Services Administration, Center for Mental Health Services, National Institutes of Health, National Institute of Mental Health.

7. Hassed, C. (2006). *Mind-Body Medicine: Science, Practice and Philosophy*. Lecture notes, Dept of General Practice, Monash University, October.

8. Cross, D.G. (2010). *Stopping Your Self-sabotage: Steps to Increase Your Self-confidence.* Crossways Publishing

9. Cross, D.G. (2008). *Growing Up Children: How to Get 5-12 Year Olds To Behave & Do As They're Told.* Crossways Publishing.

CHAPTER 6 REFERENCES

1. American Psychological Association (APA). (1998)."How Psychotherapy Helps People Recover from Depression," 1998. https://www.apa.org/practice/programs/campaign/fyi-depression.pdf

2. (NIMH) U.S. Department of Health and Human Services (1999). *Mental Health: A Report of the Surgeon General.* Rockville, MD: U.S. Department of Health and Human Services, Substance Abuse and Mental Health Services Administration, Center for Mental Health Services, National Institutes of Health, National Institute of Mental Health.

3. Parker, G (2004). *Dealing with Depression.* Crows Nest, NSW: Allen & Unwin.

4. Robinson, N (2023). "Genetics on Track to Personalise Mental Health Medicines", *The Australian*, April 15.

5. Santarsieri, D & Schwartz, T.L (2015). Antidepressant efficacy and side-effect burden: A quick guide for clinicians, *Drugs Context,* 4, 212290

6. National Health Service (UK). "Side Effects – Antidepressants". https://www.nhs.uk/mental-health/talking-therapies-medicine-treatments/medicines-and-psychiatry/antidepressants/side-effects/

7. Murkherjee S. (2012). Post-prozac nation: the science and history of treating depression. *The New York Times (Sunday Magazine),* April 19

8. Al-Harbi, K.S. (2012). Treatment-resistant depression: Therapeutic trends, challenges, and future directions". https://www.ncbi.nlm.nih.gov/pmc/articles/PMC3363299/#

9. Compton, M.T. & Kotwicki, R.J. (2007). *Responding to Individuals With Mental Illnesses.* Sudbury, Massachusetts: Jones & Bartlett Publishers, Inc.

10. Miller, D.M., Lipsedge, M., Litchfield, P. Editors. (2002). *Work and Mental Health, An Employer's Guide.* London: The Royal College of Psychiatrists, 2002.

11. Gautam, M., Tripathi, A., Deshmukh, D., & Gaur, M. (2020). "Cognitive Behavioral Therapy for Depression", *Indian Journal of Psychiatry, 62,* 223-229.

12. Markowitz, J.C., & Weissman, M.M. (2004). "Interpersonal psychotherapy: principles and applications", *World Psychiatry, 3(3),* 136-139.

13. Mayo Clinic. Electroconvulsive therapy (ECT). https://www.mayoclinic.org/tests-procedures/electroconvulsive-therapy/about/pac-20393894

14. The New York Times (October 10, 2000) "Exercise Found Effective Against Depression". https://www.nytimes.com/2000/10/10/health/exercise-found-effective-against-depression.html

15. Tan, G., Shaffer, F., Lyle, R, Teo, I, and Lyle, R.R. (2016). *Evidence-based Practice in Biofeedback and Neurofeedback* (3rd Ed)., Association for Applied Psychophysiology and Biofeedback

16. Davis, M., Eshelman, E.R., & McKay, M. (1995). *The Relaxation & Stress Reduction Workbook* (4th Ed). New Harbinger Publications, Inc.

17. National Center for Complementary and Integrative Health. "St John's Wort and Depression: In depth". https://www.nccih.nih.gov/health/st-johns-wort-and-depression-in-depth

18. Wilson, D.R. (2022). "Can essential oils treat depression?" *Medical News Today*. https://www.medicalnewstoday.com/articles/315481

CHAPTER 7 REFERENCES

1. Collins, R.L. (2006). Depression in primary care. Managing Obstacles to Improved Outcomes in Depression. Supplement to *Managed Care, 15* (10), 3-4.

2. Kessler, R.C., Greenberg, P.E. & Mickelson, K.D. (2001). The effects of chronic medical conditions on work loss and work cutback. *Journal Occupational Environmental Medicine, 43*, 218-225.

3. Miller, Doreen M., Lipsedge, Maurice, Litchfield, Paul, Editors (2002). *Work and Mental Health, An Employer's Guide*. The Royal College of Psychiatrists.

4. Goff, C.V. (2006). Depression in the Workplace. *Managed Care Magazine,1*, Spring issue.

5. Beck, A.T., Steer, R.A. & Garbin, M.G. (1988). Psychometric properties on the Beck Depression Inventory: Twenty-five years of evaluation. *Clinical Psychology Review, 8*, 77-100.

6. Beck, A.T., Steer, R.A., & Brown, G.K. (1996). *BDI-II Beck Depression Inventory: Manual.* 2nd edition. Boston: Harcourt Brace.

7. Radloff, L.S. (1977). The CES-D scale: A self-report depression scale for research in the general population. *Applied Psychological Measurement, 1*, 385-401.

8. Zung, W.W. (1965). A self-rating depression scale. *Archives of General Psychiatry, 12*, 63-70.

CHAPTER 8 REFERENCES

1. Wang, P.S., Simon, G.E., Avorn, J., Azocar, F., Ludman, E.J., McCulloch, J., Petukhova, M.Z., & Kessler, R.C. (2007). Telephone screening, outreach and care management for depressed workers and impact on clinical and work productivity outcomes, a randomized controlled trial. *Journal of the American Medical Association, 298* (12), 1401-11.

2. Beaton Consulting. (2007). http://www.beaton.com.au/pdfs/BC_ProfessionsSurvey.pdf

3. American Psychological Association (APA). (2004, 2006). "Workplace Survey."

CHAPTER 9 REFERENCES

1. Cross, D.G. (2019). *You're a New Leader: So Now What?* Crossways Publishing

CHAPTER 10 REFERENCES

1. Massand, P.S. (2003). "Tolerability and adherence issues in antidepressant therapy," *Clinical Therapeutics, Volume 25*, (8), pages 2289-2304.

2. Lee, J.K., Grace, K.A. & Taylor A.J. (2006). Effect of a pharmacy care program on medication adherence and

persistence, blood pressure, and low-density lipoprotein cholesterol. *Journal of the American Medical Association, 296,* pages 2563-2571   http://jama.ama-assn.org/cgi/content/full/296/21/2563?maxtoshow=&HITS=10&hits=10&RESULTFORMAT=&fulltext=Federal+Study+of+Adherence+to+Medications+in+the+Elderly+%28FAME%29+Study&searchid=1&FIRSTINDEX=0&resourcetype=HWCIT

CHAPTER 11 REFERENCES

1. Cross, D.G. (2017). *Listen Up Now: How to Increase Growth and Profit by Really Listening to Your Customers and Clients.* Crossways Publishing

CHAPTER 12 REFERENCES

1. Gilbreath B., & Benson P.G. (2004). The contribution of supervisor behavior to employee psychological well-being. *Work & Stress,* 18, (3).

2. Boyatzis, R.E., & McKee, A. (2005) *Resonant Leadership,* Harvard Business School Press.

CHAPTER 13 REFERENCES

1. Cross, D.G. (2017). *Listen Up Now: How to Increase Growth and Profit by Really Listening to Your Customers and Clients.* Crossways Publishing

CHAPTER 14 REFERENCES

1. Australian Human Rights Commission. "Mental Health in the Workplace". Website retrieved 12 January, 2023.

https://humanrights.gov.au/our-work/1-mental-health-workplace

2. U.S. Dept. of Justice (Civil Rights Division). "Americans with Disabilities Act of 1990," Website retrieved 12 January, 2023. https://www.ada.gov/law-and-regs/ada/

Appendix A:

Clinical Criteria for Major Depressive Episode

The symptoms which warrant a diagnosis of major depressive episode are:

A. In the same two-week period, the person has had **five or more** of the following symptoms, which are a definite change from usual functioning. *Either depressed mood or decreased interest or pleasure must be one of the five.*

- **Mood.** For most of nearly every day, the person reports depressed mood (e.g., feels sad or empty) or appears depressed to others (e.g., appears tearful). Note: In children and adolescents, this symptom can present as irritable mood.

- **Interests.** For most of nearly every day, interest or pleasure is markedly decreased in nearly all activities (as noted by the person or by others), including activities that the person normally enjoys doing. The person may lose interest in work, hobbies and sexual activity.

- **Eating and weight.** Although the person is not dieting, there is a marked loss or gain of weight (such as 5% in one month), or appetite is markedly decreased or increased nearly every day.

- **Sleep.** Nearly every day, the person sleeps excessively or not enough (insomnia or hypersomnia). Even if sleeping excessively, the person often still feels tired.

- **Observable psychomotor activity.** Nearly every day, others can see that the person's activity is speeded up or slowed down.

- **Fatigue.** Nearly every day, there is tiredness or loss of energy.

- **Self-worth.** Nearly every day, the person feels worthless or inappropriately guilty. These feelings are not just about being sick; they may be delusional.

- **Concentration.** As noted by the person or by others, nearly every day the person is indecisive, or has trouble thinking or concentrating.

- **Death.** The person has had repeated thoughts about death (other than the fear of dying), or about suicide (with or without a plan), or has made a suicide attempt.

B. To warrant a diagnosis of major depressive episode, the episode must be severe enough to cause material distress or impairment in the individual's work performance or social life.

C. The person doesn't fulfill the criteria for a mixed episode — the coexistence of symptoms of mania and depression within the same time period.

D. **Substance exclusion.** Regardless of the severity or duration of the symptoms, major depressive episode should not be diagnosed if the disorder is directly caused by a general medical condition, or by the use of substances, including prescription medications.

E. **Bereavement exclusion.** Major depressive episode

should not be diagnosed if the episode began within two months of the loss of a loved one (bereavement). There is, however, an exclusion for the bereavement exclusion: If the symptoms are unusually severe, a major depressive episode may be diagnosed regardless of the time elapsed since the death of a friend or relative. Examples of severity might include: severely impaired functioning, severe preoccupation with worthlessness, ideas of suicide, delusions or hallucinations, or slowed psychomotor activity.

Appendix B

Clinical Criteria for Manic Episode

The criteria which warrants a diagnosis of manic episode are:

A. For at least one week (or less if the patient has to be hospitalised), the patient's mood is abnormally and persistently high, irritable or expansive.

B. To a material degree during this time, the patient has persistently had three or more of these symptoms (four if the only abnormality of mood is irritability):

1) Grandiosity or exaggerated self-esteem.

2) Reduced need for sleep.

3) Increased talkativeness, pressure to keep talking.

4) Flight of ideas or racing thoughts.

5) Easy distractibility, i.e. their attention is too easily drawn to unimportant or irrelevant external stimuli.

6) Speeded-up psychomotor activity or increased goal-directed activity (such as social, school or work).

7) Poor judgment and excessive involvement in pleasurable activities that have a high potential for painful consequences, for example, spending sprees, sexual indiscretions, or foolish business investments.

C. The person doesn't fulfill the criteria for a mixed episode — the coexistence of symptoms of mania and depression within the same time period.

D. To warrant a diagnosis of manic episode, the mood disturbance must be severe enough to cause marked impairment in the individual's occupational and social functioning or to necessitate hospitalisation to prevent harm to self and others, or there are psychotic features.

E. The symptoms are not due to the direct physiological effects of a general medical condition or the use of substances, including prescription medications.

Appendix C

Anti-depressant Drugs Currently Available According to Generation Released

	Drug name
First generation antidepressants	
Tricyclics (TCAs)	Amitriptyline
	Clomipramine
	Dothiepin
	Doxepin
	Imipramine
	Nortriptyline
	Trimipramine
Irreversible monoamine oxidaze inhibitors (MAOIs)	Phenelzine
	Tranylcypromine
Second generation antidepressants	
Tetracyclics	Mianserin
Third generation antidepressants	
Selective serotonin reuptake inhibitors (SSRIs)	Citalopram
	Escitalopram
	Fluvoxamine
	Fluoxetine
	Paroxetine
	Sertraline
Serotonin and noradrenaline reuptake inhibitors (SNRIs)	Duloxetine
	Venlafaxine
5-HT2 blockers	Nefazodone
Reversible inhibitors of monoamine oxidase-A (RIMAs)	Moclobemide
Other drug types	
Noradrenaline reuptake inhibitors (NARIs)	Reboxetine
Dopamine-noradrenaline reuptake inhibitors (DNRIs)	Bupropion
Noradrenergic and specific serotonergic antidepressants (NaSSAs)	Mirtazapine

Appendix D

Anti-depressant Treatments; Classes, Side Effects, and Prescribing Considerations

Classes, SEs, and prescribing considerations for ADT.

Class	Drugs	SE	Considerations
TCA	Imipramine Amitriptyline Doxepin Desipramine Nortriptyline	Weight gain, sedation, dry mouth, nausea, blurred vision, constipation, tachycardia	Generally not first-line therapy due to increased anticholinergic and cardiotoxic SE
MAOI	Isocarboxazid Phenelzine Tranylcypromine Selegiline	Weight gain, fatigue, sexual dysfunction, hypotension	Generally not first-line therapy due to serotonin syndrome and hypertensive crises
SSRI	Fluoxetine Paroxetine Sertraline Citalopram Escitalopram	Headaches, GI distress, insomnia, fatigue, anxiety, sexual dysfunction, weight gain	Often first-line treatment due to safer SE profile. Subtle SE differences must be weighed by the prescriber
SNRI	Venlafaxine Desvenlafaxine Duloxetine Levomilnacipran	Nausea, insomnia, dry mouth, headache, increased blood pressure, sexual dysfunction, weight gain	SEs are similar to but may be slightly more frequent than with SSRI
Atypical	Bupropion	Headache, agitation, insomnia, loss of appetite, weight loss, sweating	Increased seizure risk in eating disorder and epilepsy patients. No sexual dysfunction or weight gain. May also help to quit smoking
	Mirtazapine	Sedation, increased appetite, weight gain	Sedation may be less with higher dose. Much reduced nausea and sexual dysfunction compared with SSRI/SNRI. Some risk of reduced white blood cell count
	Trazodone	Sedation, nausea, priapism (rare)	Lower risk of weight gain and sexual dysfunction, but may cause priapism. Often used to induce sleep as a positive effect
	Vilazodone	Nausea, diarrhea, insomnia	Better SE profile than most ADTs with lower risk of sexual dysfunction or weight gain
	Vortioxetine	Nausea, diarrhea, dizziness	Similar SE profile to the SSRI. May have precognitive benefits in adults with MDD

ADT, antidepressant treatment; MAOI, monoamine oxidase inhibitor; MDD, major depressive disorder; SE, side effect; SNRI, serotonin norepinephrine reuptake inhibitor; SSRI, selective serotonin reuptake inhibitor; TCA, tricyclic antidepressant.

Sourced from:
https://www.ncbi.nlm.nih.gov/pmc/articles/PMC4630974/table/t1-dic-4-212290/?report=objectonly

Appendix E

Further Information

You can call or write to any of these organizations for free information on depression. You can also find more information on their websites. "Free call" phone numbers can be used free by anyone in the United States, and 1800 or 1300 numbers in Australia, for example, means you can call anywhere for the cost of a local call. Other countries have similar arrangements.

Beyond Blue
Postal Address: PO Box 6100,
Hawthorn West
Victoria Australia 3123
Info Line: 1300 22 4636
Website: http://www.beyondblue.org.au

Lifeline Australia
Located in Capital cities and regional areas
National Office: PO Box R1084
Royal Exchange NSW 1225
Phone: (02) 6215 9400
Crisis Support Line: 13 11 14
Website: https://www.lifeline.org.au

Headspace (Mental Health for Young People)
Phone: (03) 9027 0100
Website: https://headspace.org.au

SANE
National Office: PO Box 1226,
Carlton VIC 3053
Website: www.sane.org

Head to Head
Coordinates digital mental health services from some of Australia's most trusted mental health organisations
Website: https://www.headtohealth.gov.au

MensLine Australia
Postal: On the Line, PO Box 2335
Footscray VIC 3011
Phone: 1300 78 99 78
Website: https://mensline.org.au

National Institute of Mental Health (NIMH)
Office of Communications and Public Liaison
Information Resources and Inquiries Branch
6001 Executive Boulevard
Room 8184, MSC 9663
Bethesda MD USA 20892-9663
Free call: 1-800 -421 4211
Local call: 301 443 4513
Hearing impaired: (TTY): 301-443-8431
Website: http://www.nimh.nih.gov
Email: nimhinfo@nih.gov

National Alliance for the Mentally Ill (NAMI)
Suite 300
2107 Wilson Boulevard
Arlington VA USA 22201-3042
Free call: 1-800-950-6264
Local call: 703-524-7600

Depression & Bipolar Support Alliance
Suite 501
730 N. Franklin Street
Chicago IL USA 60601-7204
Free call: 1-800-826-3632
Local call: 312-642-0049
Website: http://www.ndmda.org

National Foundation for Depressive Illness Inc (NAFDI)
PO Box 2257
New York NY USA 10116
Free call: 1-800-239-1265
Local call: 212-268-4260
Website: http://www.depression.org

National Mental Health Association (NMHA)
12th Floor
2001 N. Beauregard Street
Alexandria VA USA 22311
Free call: 1-800-969-6642
Local call: 703-684-7722
Free all: hearing impaired (TTY): 1-800-433-5959
Website: http://www.nmha.org

Depression Alliance
212 Spitfire Studios, 63-71 Collier Street, London N1 9BE
Local call: 0845 123 23 20
Website: http://www.depressionalliance.org

Saneline (United Kingdom)
Local call: 0845 767 8000
Website: http://www.sane.org.uk

The British Association of Behavioural and Cognitive Psychotherapies (BABCP)
Globe Centre, PO BOX 9, Accrington, UK BB5 2GD
Local call: 01254 875277
Website: http://www.babcp.com

ABOUT THE AUTHOR

CROSSWAYS CONSULTING

Dr. DARRYL CROSS PhD (Psychology)

Psychologist & Leadership Coach

Fellow, Australian Psychological Society
Fellow, College of Clinical Psychologists
Fellow, College of Organisational Psychologists
Fellow, Institute of Managers and Leaders
Certified Personal & Executive Coach, College of Exec Coaching
Certified Mentor Coach, College of Executive Coaching
Graduate, Australian Institute of Company Directors
Member, Institute of Coaching
Member, International Coaching Federation
Accredited Advisor, Family Business Australia
International Member, American Psychological Association
Registered Psychologist

Dr. Darryl Cross is both a **clinical and organisational psychologist** as well as a personal and executive coach, along with being an author, speaker and former university lecturer.

Darryl completed his Psychology Honours Degree in Psychology at Flinders University, South Australia. He gained his Doctorate in Psychology from the University of Queensland.

More recently, Darryl completed a Professional Development Certificate in Coaching Practice through the Department of Psychology at the University of Sydney, and then completed graduate studies in coaching with the College of Executive Coaching (CEC) in California, USA as well as being an accredited Mentor Coach from the CEC.

He **knows how organisations work** from his first appointment for three years as an Occupational Psychologist with the Australian Federal Government, and then as a director of a hospital department in Adelaide before starting his own consulting business over twenty-five years ago.

As a **university lecturer**, he tutored and lectured in psychology at the University of Queensland in Brisbane for seven years, and lectured in the post-graduate Masters programs in psychology at Macquarie University in Sydney, New South Wales for three years. He was formerly a sessional lecturer in "Leadership Dynamics" in the MBA Program in the International Graduate School of Business at the University of South Australia followed by a similar course at Torrens University.

As a **speaker**, Darryl has conducted countless workshops on numerous topics including, the Art of Listening, Coaching for Managers, Leadership, Dealing with Burn-out, Building Resilience and Creating Positive Cultures. He has spoken internationally at numerous conferences and symposia and presented workshops in countries such as the United Kingdom and the USA, and in South-east Asia.

As an **author**, Darryl has published numerous papers for national and overseas academic journals, as well as articles for the popular press.

He has also authored books such as *"You're a New Leader: So Now What"*, *"Stopping Your Self-Sabotage: Steps to Increase Your Self-Confidence"*, and *"Listen Up Now! How to Increase Profit and Growth in Business by Really Listening to Your Clients & Customers"*.

He is heard regularly on talk-back radio and is often seen on various segments on television as well as in the print media. He knows what he's talking about and is called upon to give his opinion.

Academic study, as well as life experience and being a psychologist and coach for over forty years means that Dr. Cross has come up with practical ways to use principles of life that work. He understands human behaviour and therefore can help individuals and teams to move to another place. He has the knack of being able to say it all simply.

Address: Crossways Consulting
PO Box 2000,
North Adelaide
South Australia
AUSTRALIA   5006

Email: enquiries@crossways.com.au

www.DrDarryl.com
www.LeadershipCoaching.com.au
www.NewLeader.com.au
www.SuccessPursuit.com
www.HowToStopSelfSabotage.com
www.ListenUpNow.com.au
www.FindACareerPath.com
www.MyFutureCareer.com.au
www.GrowingUpChildren.com
www.TeenagerTroubleShooting.com

www.ingramcontent.com/pod-product-compliance
Lightning Source LLC
Chambersburg PA
CBHW072050020426
42334CB00017B/1449